FOCUSED for TENNIS

KARL SLAIKEU, PhD

ROBERT TROGOLO

Human Kinetics

Library of Congress Cataloging-in-Publication Data

Skaikeu, Karl A., 1944-
  Focused for tennis / Karl Slaikeu, Robert Trogolo.
      p.   cm.
   Includes bibliographical references (p. 131) and index.
   ISBN 0-88011-722-2 (paperback)
      1. Tennis--Psychological aspects.   I. Trogolo, Robert, 1953-   .
II. Title.
GV1002.9.P75S59   1998
796.342'01'9--dc21   98-12620
                                                                    CIP

ISBN: 0-88011-722-2

Acquisitions Editor: Martin Barnard; **Developmental Editor:** Jim Kestner; **Managing Editor:** Joanna Hatzopoulos; **Assistant Editor:** Jennifer Miller; **Copyeditor:** Stephen Moore; **Proofreader:** Jim Burns; **Indexer:** Vita Richman for Writers Anonymous, Inc.; **Graphic Designer:** Fred Starbird; **Graphic Artist:** Francine Hamerski; **Photo Editor:** Boyd LaFoon; **Cover Designer:** Jack Davis; **Photographer (cover):** ©Robert Skeoch; **Photographer (interior):** All photos by Jim Sigmon unless otherwise indicated; **Illustrator:** Chuck Nivens; **Printer:** United Graphics

Human Kinetics books are available at special discounts for bulk purchase. Special editions or book excerpts can also be created to specifications. For details, contact the Special Sales Manager at Human Kinetics.

Printed in the United States of America   10   9   8   7   6   5   4   3   2

Human Kinetics
Web site: http://www.humankinetics.com/

United States: Human Kinetics
P.O. Box 5076
Champaign, IL 61825-5076
1-800-747-4457
e-mail: humank@hkusa.com

Canada: Human Kinetics, Box 24040
Windsor, ON N8Y 4Y9
1-800-465-7301 (in Canada only)
e-mail: humank@hkcanada.com

Europe: Human Kinetics, P.O. Box IW14
Leeds LS16 6TR, United Kingdom
(44) 1132 781708
e-mail: humank@hkeurope.com

Australia: Human Kinetics
57A Price Avenue
Lower Mitcham, South Australia 5062
(088) 277 1555
e-mail: humank@hkaustralia.com

New Zealand: Human Kinetics
P.O. Box 105-231, Auckland 1
(09) 523 3462
e-mail: humank@hknewz.com

Contents

Foreword

I have played a lot of matches in my career where I have lost to myself. My anger and frustration consumed me. I lost concentration and was no longer able to focus on what I had to do. This is how I know that learning to rid yourself of negative emotions is one of the most important things you as a tennis player can do to improve your performance.

The Three R's is an excellent tool that will help any player deal with the past point and prepare mentally for the next. When things are not going well, it's easy to get "down" on yourself and play negatively. By using the Three R's, you can stay positive and focused regardless of the result of any one point or game. Any tennis match is rewarding when you are able to play with a clear head.

Both Karl Slaikeu and Robert Trogolo offer very unique perspectives to players at all levels. Karl Slaikeu brings his experience as a sport psychologist, player, and tennis parent. The psychological principles behind the Three R's are sound. They are also practical and logical—you don't have to have a PhD to "get" the Three R's. Robert Trogolo knows the mental and physical strains we tennis players go through; not only has he coached several players on the tour like Michael Chang, Richey Reneberg, and Luke Smith, he has played on the tour himself. The result of both Slaikeu's and Trogolo's perspectives is a book that works in theory and in practice. And thanks to its simplicity, you can easily remember the Three R's and incorporate them into the short time period allotted between points.

So when you're out there working on your serve or your backhand volley, don't forget to work on your mental game as well. Reading about the Three R's is the first step to becoming a mentally tough tennis player. It can help any level of player at any age. The sooner you learn good mental habits, the better you will be.

Wayne Ferreira
January, 1998

Preface

This book is for every tennis player who wants to move up to the next level of play. Written by a sport psychologist and a veteran of the pro tour, it helps players build successful strategies on a simple yet often neglected premise: What you do when the ball is out of play can be just as important as what you do when you hit the ball—if not more so.

You needn't look far to test this premise yourself. In tennis and in life, the way we *think* about things—whether we encourage ourselves or knock ourselves down—can make the critical difference between success and failure. When you are playing badly, you can make things worse by berating yourself. (Say "You're terrible!" often enough and you start to believe it—and make it true.) Frustrations and distractions can make you forget your game plan.

This book describes a powerful system that will let you solve this problem and unlock your best tennis. We first developed it with highly competitive players, then shared it with players at all levels. The message they brought back was loud and clear: "This works! I wish I'd been doing it earlier!" The system teaches you to focus your thoughts and behavior during the 25 seconds between points when the ball is out of play, and also during the 90 seconds at changeovers. It also works between matches—the time during the week when you are not playing, but are thinking ahead to a match.

THE THREE R'S SYSTEM

Sport psychologist Jim Loehr first studied the way top tennis players used their time between points to collect themselves, to relax, and to go through various behavioral routines to prepare for either serving or returning. His article in *World Tennis* (February, 1990) still provides useful insight on the importance of between-point activity in tennis. Our system builds on this early work, and psychology studies of "off-task" behavior for individuals and groups. We use the "STOP" technique from clinical psychology and several other sport psychology tools. Compared with other approaches, our system is shorter and easier to remember. And, as players at all levels have found, it works! (See the references at the back of the book.)

Here's how it goes: The system teaches you to *Release* your reaction to the point you just finished, so you can go forward fresh and ready. Then it helps you to *Review* where you are in the match, check your game plan, and use key images and code words to help you focus, after which you *Reset* yourself with a behavioral routine that helps you get ready to put the ball in play or return serve. We call this the Three R's—Release, Review, and Reset. You will find that you can apply the system between points and at changeovers and also to other areas of your life. In the course of teaching the Three R's system around the world, we have had many players tell us they use it to succeed in activities as diverse as business negotiations, standardized tests, and other sports such as golf, soccer, baseball, and basketball.

OUR PERSONAL PLEDGE

We love the game of tennis, and we love to help anyone who wants to improve. Our backgrounds include a range of experience with the game. Slaikeu first started to play after learning how to hold a racket from instructions in the *World Book Encyclopedia*, and then practiced hitting against the wall in a church basement. Trogolo came up through the junior competitive ranks, spent several years on the pro tour, and then coached players such as Michael Chang, Kevin Curren, and Richie Rennenberg, as well as the Malaysian Davis Cup team. These days we work with players at all levels, some new to the game and others who want more than anything else to beat one special person who has been giving them trouble for years. We have not found a player who cannot get better by improving mental focus—and for us, the Three R's system offers the best path to this goal. We are excited about the opportunity to bring our system to you through the pages of this book.

Acknowledgments

We are indebted to the numerous players and coaches who have assisted us in testing and refining the Three R's system over the past several years. We give particular thanks to: Diane Slaikeu for helping us bring conceptual clarity to the three phases, and for drawing on her experience as a tennis parent and tennis spouse in making the system user-friendly; Ingrid Ramsey and Hilary Powers for their assistance in editing the manuscript and to Robert Dole for his help with the player profiles and numerous other production tasks. Special thanks to Ann Blackwood, Natalie Pham, Luke Smith, Kristina Slaikeu, Micah Thompson, and Jamin Thompson for helping with photos to illustrate the Three R's System.

Karl A. Slaikeu, Ph.D.
Robert Trogolo
September, 1996

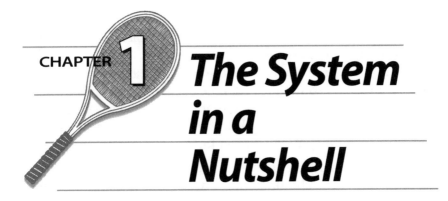

CHAPTER **1**

The System in a Nutshell

What do you do between points? For every hour in a tennis match, the ball is in play only 4 to 15 of the total 60 minutes. This means that you spend less than one-fourth of your time hitting the ball, and three-fourths or more walking around, toweling off, and thinking. Perhaps you spend some of that time looking off to the side, letting your mind wander to something unrelated to the task at hand. Or you might be thinking ahead to the next point. If you have problems maintaining your focus, you may be committing one or more of the "seven deadly sins" of between-point tennis. See if any of these apply to you.

1. **Exploding.** You do not handle frustration well. You have a hair trigger and sometimes blow up between points. When you aren't playing well you throw your racket, hit the ball against the screen, or condemn yourself (and the world, and the heavens) loudly and perhaps profanely. Sometimes you regain your focus, but often the intense feelings of the explosion spill over into the next point. Instead of improving your play, all that energy makes you play worse.

2. **Holding it in.** This is the opposite of exploding. You think of yourself as the strong, silent type, but the inner you often churns on the tennis court. You do not show your feelings, but keep them bottled up inside. Meanwhile, your body gets tense, sometimes so tense you can't execute shots properly. At its worst,

your control turns to a choke. You would like to let it out, but you do not know how to do so in a good way.

3. **Rushing.** You play fast. Sometimes too fast. Your speed is okay when you are playing well, but when you are playing badly, you rush your serve, sometimes double fault, and things start to go downhill. You sometimes "donate" points and games by making unforced errors one after another. When it is bad, it gets very bad. You would like to slow down and collect yourself, but you do not do so when you most need to.

4. **Not thinking.** You have told yourself to get your first serve in, or to turn your shoulders more when executing a forehand, but you forget to do it. You are not winning the big points when you need to. You get so caught up in the action, or so worried about the outcome ("I can't let this guy beat me!") that you don't think. Sometimes after a match you wonder: "What was I doing out there?" Fact is, you do not know.

5. **Catastrophizing.** It's not just the game of tennis. It's not just the point. It's not just the double fault. It's life! After all, tennis *is* life, and when you play badly, you want to pack it in! Something small becomes something large and catastrophic. You cannot seem to stop yourself.

6. **Wandering.** You have no pattern for what you do between points. You wander over to pick up the ball, move to the line to serve, look at your opponent, and put the ball in play. Sometimes you bounce the ball two times, other times once, and on other occasions you give it six bounces. There is no pattern to it, and you are not sure what the pattern should be like even if you wanted one.

7. **Sleeping.** You don't actually close your eyes, lie down, and go to sleep—but it sometimes seems that way. You simply are not in the game. Your mind goes someplace else. It seems as if you want to withdraw. Maybe the prospect of losing to this opponent is so frightening that you want to get out of there, and one way to do so is to act as if you are sleepily going through the motions. Or perhaps you did have a bad night's sleep and it shows. The problem is that you do not have a way to snap yourself out of it and bring out your best between points.

ROBERT REMEMBERS

As I read over the list of the seven deadly sins that Karl and I put together for this chapter, I have vivid memories of players falling prey to every one of them. Start off with *exploding*.

I once saw a doubles match in which a player got hit hard by an overhead and took a few seconds to get going again. The umpire gave him a warning for delay of game. The player proceeded to tell the umpire where to go. The umpire said, "Game," (defaulting that game). The player said, "#!?*!#?! you, you, #!?*!#?!" and the umpire said, "Match!"

Catastrophizing is another favorite with many players. It is not just a bad game, or a bad set, but the whole world goes to hell in a handcart. I can remember sitting in the stands, about 100 feet from the court, as my guy walked over and held his hands up in the air, shaking them and looking at me as if to say, "I don't know what to do. Why is this happening to *me*?" Juniors do this a lot, saying negative things like "I'm so stupid. I can't believe how bad I am." They jump directly from a bad point or a bad game to a "bad me."

Not thinking reminds me of one of my players who lost a match at the U.S. Pro Indoors to a player with whom he was on really bad terms—these guys hated each other and called each other every name in the book throughout the match—and when my guy played the same player in the next tournament, he could not forget the previous match. We had a game plan, but he could not focus on it. In the second match he was up a set and a break, but lost the match. My impression was that he actually relived the previous match and could not get it out of his mind.

And then there is *sleeping*. If I had a nickel for every player I have seen who wanders on the court and drops the first set, deciding to wake up and get into the match in the second set when he suddenly realizes he has to win, I would be a rich man. I now tell my players to use the Three R's to get ready to win the first point, game, and set. It's easier to stay ahead than to catch up!

YOU MIGHT NOT BE AS CRAZY AS YOU THINK!

Don't think yourself too strange if you are guilty of one or more of these sins. We all fall into them at one time or another. As a matter of fact, psychologists have found these same sins crop up predictably in both individual and group behavior in all sorts of fields. Whenever people put aside the task at hand, they tend to be more susceptible to negative thinking and behavior than when they are engaged in the task. You see the same phenomenon between points in tennis.

Have a look at the two columns in table 1.1. On the left is a summary of the research on individuals and groups, and the characteristics of what can happen to any of us during off-task activity, whether at school, at work, or in sport. On the right is the between-point version that shows what can happen to us on the tennis court. As a quick glance shows, the following can strike any of us during the in-between time: A rise in self-defeating behavior, a drop in self-esteem, or a derailment of dedication and drive leading to frustration. It is normal under stress—in the off-task time—to look back at the problems instead of looking forward to what you need to do next. It is normal when you are under stress to have a difficult time planning your next move. At times, your thoroughness and the quality of what you are doing can decrease, leading to unforced errors. Muscles tighten up and executing shots can become a problem. You become susceptible to a choke.

THE THREE R'S

Figure 1.1 gives a visual summary of the Three R's system. The system shows three events, each customized to your own personality, that will occur between each point: *Release* (followed by a STOP), *Review* (followed by another STOP), and then a *Reset* routine, after which you put the ball in play. As we shall see, you can learn to take charge of any situation between points by channeling your thoughts, feelings, and behavior through these three phases.

Think of it this way: The point is over, and you have 25 seconds or so before you serve or return. Picture this time as your opportunity to react appropriately to what just happened (whether it was

Table 1.1 "Off Task" Psychology

Psychologists researching individual and group behavior have iden-tified several predictable hazards during "off task" activity, which we can compare to "between point" time in tennis. In the table be-low, we have listed the characteristics of individuals and groups during non-work or off-task activity to the left, and the between point tennis version to the right.

Psychology Research on Individuals/Groups	Between Point Tennis Version
Members devote energy to self-defeating ends.	You engage in verbal self-abuse, or throw your racket.
Self-esteem decreases.	Your self-talk becomes negative: "You're terrible!," "You can't play!," "You should quit!"
Drive and dedication in the face of constraints lead to frustration and burnout in highly motivated and com-mitted individuals.	The more you want to win, the more frustrated you are when you play badly.
Foresight becomes hindsight.	You keep looking back instead of ahead. You're down only one break, but you can't get it out of your mind that you had break points and blew it!
Predictive capacity decreases.	You are so upset that you can't think ahead.
Thoroughness and quality decreases.	You make unforced errors.
The work climate deteriorates.	At its worst, the court feels like a disaster scene for your game.

(continued)

Table 1.1, (continued)

Psychology Research on Individuals/Groups	Between Point Tennis Version
Perception narrows.	You can't get the negatives out of your mind, and can't broaden the horizon to see where you are in the match and what needs to be done next.
Manual support systems deteriorate.	Your muscles tighten up; you can't execute your shots, and you choke.

a rather uneventful point, a wild success, or a major disappointment), check where you are in your game plan and what you want to do next, and Reset your mind and muscles for the next point. That is, Release the previous point, Review where you stand, and Reset for the next point. It doesn't take long to run through the Three R's—and, after all, if you weren't doing the Three R's, you'd be doing something else. Probably something less constructive for your game. Let's have a brief look at each phase.

First R: Release

The Release is a letting go of the point that has just been completed. Sometimes the Release is very mild, as in the early going of any match, when you finish hitting a good shot and simply turn away from the ball and say or think to yourself, "All right!" No one really notices that you are conducting a Release. You have simply made a positive statement to yourself about the point just completed. At other times, the Release may be wide open to the public. For example, making fun of yourself after missing a shot is a form of Release. Releases can be positive or negative. If you are feeling good, then the Release will be positive, perhaps a fist pump or some other affirmation of what just happened. If you are playing badly and are upset, nervous, or angry, a Release might take the form of saying something out loud—though it's best to train yourself to make statements that don't invite code violations. The best Releases in situations in which you aren't playing well are those where you immediately imitate the shot you wish you had made. For example, if you fail to turn when you volley and instead hit the ball with your shoulders square to the net, sailing it long, you might immediately fix it—that is, turn, take an appropriate step toward the net, and hit an imaginary

ball properly. This is an example of a constructive Release aimed at letting go of negative energy by channeling it in a constructive direction.

Second R: Review

The next phase is Review, in which you think about what just happened and make plans for how you will play the next point. For example, you might switch your racket to your other hand, walk toward the baseline, and think something along the lines of: "What just happened? Did I make an unforced error, or is my

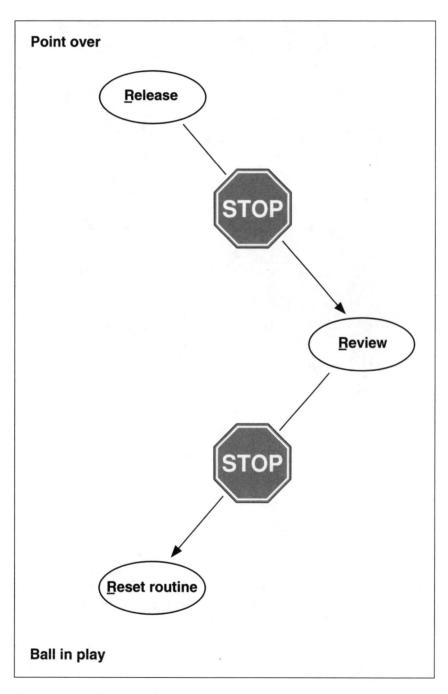

Figure 1.1   The Three Rs: Sequence

opponent outplaying me? Do I need to change anything in my game plan or should I stay with what I am doing?" This is also the time when you will remind yourself of your own game plan, perhaps with code words—which we'll discuss later. Or you might say key preplanned phrases to yourself that help you focus ("First serve in, and make the first volley!").

Third R: Reset

The final R is the Reset routine you go through before serving or returning. This is a preplanned series of steps, customized to your own style of play, that will relax you (or, if needed, rev you up) before the next point. When serving, you might stand in the back court and look at your opponent, then step to the line and call the score. Then you imagine the serve you will hit, take a deep breath and exhale to relax, bounce the ball your preferred number of times, and pause before you begin the service motion. When returning serve, you may go through a sequence that in-cludes walking confidently into the return area, looking at your opponent, bouncing on your toes, and doing a split step before returning the serve. Most Reset routines will be of the relaxing type, though sometimes, if you are underaroused and cannot seem to get moving, you will need to rev up. In this case, your Reset may include slapping your thigh and saying something to your-self like "C'mon!".

The STOP Technique

Note in table 1.2 that the phases are separated from one another by the word STOP. The Three R's system uses a STOP technique to end the Release phase and keep it from spilling over into the Review. Similarly, a STOP after the Review (the thinking part) keeps it from spilling over into the Reset routine. The STOP tech-nique is borrowed from *thought stopping*, a tool clinical psy-chologists use to help patients deal with obsessive thoughts, and is a powerful way to end one behavior in the sequence and move to another. The STOP technique is discussed in more detail in chapter 2.

THE REST OF THIS BOOK

The next few chapters will give you more on each of the Three R's and will show you how to apply the system to your own game. As you read through the chapters and apply the exercises to your own situation, keep in mind that:

• *The system does not require you to change your personality.* Some people are simply more emotional than others, with a greater need to let out their feelings. Others are more private and keep things inside. That's fine. The Three R's will not change

Table 1.2   The Three R's Make a Difference

No Three R's	Using the Three R's
I play fast.	I take full advantage of the 25 seconds between points.
I let my frustrations out in negative ways, and sometimes get code violations.	I Release the negative, and then I move on.
I forget my game plan.	I Review my game plan.
I am vulnerable to choke, tank, or distraction.	I might get nervous, discouraged, or distracted, but I channel it through a Release, STOP it, then a Review so I can get back into the game effectively.
If I am down, I am down, and it is hard to get back up.	If I am down, I use the STOP and add rev up moves to my Reset routine to get going again.
I get discouraged by errors.	I correct errors as they occur, getting stronger with each point.
When I am ahead, I let down, and sometimes let my opponent back in.	When I am ahead, I use Review and Reset to stay focused and close out the match.

this basic tendency, but instead will teach you ways to handle your thoughts and feelings between points in keeping with your personality type.

• *The Three R's system does not require you to be positive all the time.* It does help you to be constructive when things go badly. Tennis is a rough-and-tumble sport, and you will sometimes get angry or frightened or depressed about it. The Three R's system teaches you to express these feelings appropriately, then to STOP and move on to the next step.

• *The Three R's system does not require you to think all the time.* You will think about where you are in the match at certain times between points, but this will not keep you from reaching the *zone*, the mental and physical space where good play flows seemingly effortlessly. Indeed, the Three R's will help you find your zone and play in it more often!

Here are some things that the system does require of you:

• *A desire to improve.* Here you are home free! If you did not have a desire to improve, you would not be reading this book. If you are like the rest of us, you know that deep inside you have some great shots and a will to win. The only problem is that you cannot hit those great shots or win on a regular basis. The very desire to bring out your best tennis is the starting point.

• *An open mind.* The standard sport psychology tools have been around for a long time, and there are not very many new ones. All we have done is repackage standard tools in a way that anyone can use. Before you decide whether the system will help you, make sure you understand all three phases (with the intervening STOP techniques), that you have customized them for personal use, and have practiced them awhile. Then let the results speak for themselves.

• *Practice.* Think of the last time a coach helped you change any part of your game. It may have involved learning a kick serve. Maybe you had to change your grip. It felt awkward at first, right? And so will the Three R's. Using the system will feel awkward at first, but this will change as you practice, practice, practice.

MICHAEL CHANG

In 1987, at age 15, Michael Chang became the youngest player to win a main draw match at the U.S. Open and ended the year ranked 163. He turned pro in 1988. In 1989, Chang was the first American male to win the French Open since Tony Trabert in 1955 and at age 17 became the youngest French Open and Grand Slam champion. By 1996 Chang compiled a 7–10 record playing against Top 10 opponents and assembled a 50–9 record on hard courts. He finished the year ranked 2 with four titles and as a finalist at the Australian and the U.S. Opens, bringing in $2,015,699 in prize money.

Michael is a swift player and has an all-court game but prefers to play baseline. He is known for his consistency on the court, regardless of his performance. If he hits a good shot, sometimes he will pump his fist. He rarely gets visibly frustrated over mistakes. His review is consistent: If he misses a forehand or backhand return, he will stroke three or four times to make sure he has a clear picture of what the correction feels like. Chang developed his tough mental edge coming up in the juniors and developed a reputation for fighting for every point.

Michael Chang was born February 22, 1972, in Hoboken, New Jersey. His parents are research chemists; his father Joe introduced him to the game and still guides his son. Chang supports grassroots tennis development in Asia through his Stars of the Future program in Hong Kong and the Reebok Challenge across Asia. Chang, an avid fisherman, often finds time to fish while traveling. He also breeds tropical fish. He is a national spokesperson for the National Fish & Wildlife Federation. He lives in Henderson, Nevada.

© Tommy Hindley

Michael Chang

CHAPTER 2

Sport Psychology Tools

The Three R's Sport Psychology System draws on many sport psychology tools, some of which may not be familiar to you. If you already know about the topics listed below, then proceed directly to chapter 3. If not, read this chapter to learn the standard techniques for channeling thoughts, feelings, and behavior both on and off the court. If you are experienced with them, you may still want to review this chapter before learning how to create your customized Three R's. Here are the tools:

1. Imagery
2. Self-talk
3. STOP technique
4. Body language
5. Relaxation
6. Humor
7. Meditation

IMAGERY

Can you picture what you ate for breakfast this morning? Can you picture yourself hitting strong ground strokes, creating a short ball, and moving in to knock the ball off for a winner? If so, you already know how to practice imagery. The clinical and sport psychology literature is filled with articles and case studies describing the use of imagery to help individuals solve problems and enhance performance in a variety of fields.

In the Three R's Sport Psychology System, imagery comes into play during the Review phase (for example, when you picture your game plan and choose which one you will carry out on the next point), and in the Reset phase (when you imagine a perfect toss, a smooth motion to hit your serve, following the ball to the net for a volley, and actually winning the point). You can practice imagery by doing the relaxation exercise described later in this chapter.

SELF-TALK

If you have been around the sport of tennis for any time at all, you know that tennis players talk to themselves. Frustrated players often say negative things to themselves, and other times they yell statements to pump themselves up: "Come on, John! Let's go!" What you might not know is that these players are practicing a psychology tool that has been studied quite extensively in clinical situations. The idea behind the tool is that as human beings we do not simply live life. Instead, we reflect on what has happened and we make statements to ourselves about what we are going through. These statements that we make (usually statements to ourselves, though sometimes made audible so others can hear them) are what psychologists refer to as *self-talk.*

Self-talk has power as a sport psychology tool because it provides the means by which you can turn an event in a positive or negative direction. You may have heard the quote from Shakespeare that it's not things themselves that are good or bad, but the thinking that makes them so. Consider an example. You are playing against an opponent you have never beaten, and after having two break points, when tied at 3–3 in the first set, you lose the game as your opponent holds serve. Do you think (or say) to yourself: "You dummy! That was your chance to break, and you blew it! Now you'll never beat him!" Or do you say: "Wow! What a disappointment! You had him, and let him go. But you *did* have him, and you can get him again!"

Notice the difference in the two statements. The first is totally negative. The second recognizes the negative, but then turns the statement in a positive direction: "You can get him again."

You can teach yourself to avoid negative self-talk and cultivate balanced self-talk instead. Negative self-talk includes words that disparage you, your play, and the entire situation, such as: "You're terrible. You'll never make it. That was ridiculous. You can't beat her. Now you'll never make it. There goes your ranking. You're a loser!"

Balanced statements are *behavioral*; they include both the negatives and the positives. They include specific behaviors such as: "That serve was terrible [not you as a person are terrible, but the behavior]. You had him, and you let him get away." The opposite of behavioral would be to make global and negative statements about yourself as a person or a player: "You are a joke!" or "You can't play at all, better quit right now!"

Because balanced statements include both negative and positive, they end on a hopeful note: "That was bad, but you're not out of it yet!" Or, "You missed the short ball, but you can work the point and create another one."

In the Three R's system, self-talk comes into play especially in the Release and Review phases, when you consider what just happened and evaluate the situation. During the Release, avoid global negatives about yourself ("you are terrible"), and replace them with specific behavioral statements ("that was terrible"). In the Review phase, be behavioral about what has just happened, and then repeat encouraging words to yourself that get you back into the game plan. For example: "You stayed back and got burned. Now is the time to get in. Let's go!"

Practice

If you would like to improve your self-talk, begin by noticing your thoughts following the events that take place during the day. Write down some of them. If you notice that you continue to put yourself down, work toward replacing negative put-downs with balanced statements that look at the good and the bad ("I had a good serve, but I missed the volley"), and then end on a constructive note. ("I'm going to make the next volley!")

In sum, self-talk ought to be both behavioral and focused on the good that just occurred as well as on the bad. This way it can set the stage for improvement.

STOP TECHNIQUE

One unique feature of the Three R's system is use of the STOP technique to keep Releases from taking over between points. Borrowed from clinical psychology (where it is called *thought stopping*), the technique is very simple. It begins with training yourself to stop whatever you are doing at the word "STOP." Ask a friend to help you. Find a quiet room, and begin counting from 1 to 20. Have your friend yell "Stop!" unexpectedly. You will find that as soon as this happens you stop counting immediately. This is an example of what you will be doing on the court, except then you will not say it out loud, but to yourself. You will use it to end the Release and later to STOP the Review and move on to the Reset phase.

Of course, you will not literally yell "Stop!" while on the court, but will simply think the word to yourself. After completing your Release, say the word STOP to yourself clearly and assertively. This means that it is time to STOP the Release, and move into the Review.

The STOP technique may seem so simple to you as to be almost trivial. But it works! And players need it. Look around on the court—you'll see many players have no mechanism for halting inappropriate behavior, and therefore let negative events carry forward into the next point, where it interferes with their play.

BODY LANGUAGE

Body language is your way of sending a message with behavior instead of words. It is also your way of putting your body through certain motions—acting, if you will—so you can improve your emotional and mental state. The classic example of this is the person who whistles in the dark to combat fear. By acting as if I am not afraid, I will mentally notice myself acting in this way, and begin to believe that perhaps I am not as afraid as I thought I was. Applied to tennis, the idea is to act strong, together, and in control, even though you might not feel it. This can throw your opponent off: Most people can't tell how you feel, and only see how you act. If your opponent sees you acting strong when believing you should be feeling weak, this sows confusion and may lead him or her to wonder: "What do I have to do to break you down?"

In a similar vein, by acting strong you send to yourself the message that you have the situation more under control than others might under similar circumstances. In the Three R's system, body language is important in all three phases. For example, in the Release, the act of imitating the shot you just missed (one of the most constructive Releases possible) is something you can train yourself to do as a way to combat frustration over missed shots. Similarly, by standing tall, switching your racket to the nonplaying hand, and looking at the strings as you walk to Review the situation, you are engaging in a behavior that says you are in control of the situation, even though you might be facing a formidable opponent. And finally, the Reset routine is made up almost entirely of positive body language (with the addition of some mental imagery). The Three R's is something that you begin and carry all the way through as a way of bringing your mind and heart to the level of focus required to play at peak performance on the next point.

Practice

If you would like to experiment with the effects of body language on your own tennis game, try acting as if you are in control between points in a practice match, even if you do not feel you are. See if you notice the result in the way you feel about yourself. As you face adversity, act as if you are in control of the situation, even though you do not feel like you are. Obviously, positive body language alone may not carry the day, although it is a critical sport psychology tool to be used in conjunction with the others listed in this chapter to help you make the Three R's system work for you.

RELAXATION

It is hard to be both uptight and relaxed at the same time—so by putting your body into a relaxed state, you combat uptight feelings. As a result, relaxation techniques are a hallmark of behavior therapy, and they're also used in other forms of self-help. The underlying principle is that people naturally tense up in the face of anxiety and fear, so one way to combat anxiety and fear is literally to relax the muscles. While this does not totally eliminate fear and anxiety, it provides a useful tool for bringing them to a level where you can make constructive use of them.

There are at least three powerful ways to relax. The first is to close your eyes and reach for a state of mental relaxation, and through self-talk and imagery tell yourself to relax.

A second way to relax is through deep breathing. Hatha yoga focuses on breathing and stretching as a form of relaxation, and tennis players can use a version of this on the court. Before doing so, you must learn the skill. Start by finding a comfortable place and closing your eyes (lying on a recliner or on a bed is best). Slowly take in air, filling the diaphragm and then the upper lungs while counting to 5, 6, or 7, hold the breath for that same period, and then slowly let it out for the same 5 to 7 counts. Do this two or three times and notice the relaxation that flows through your body. Later, you can shorten the time to a few seconds in, a few to hold the breath, and a few to let it out.

A third approach is deep muscle relaxation, first formulated by Edmund Jacobson in *You Must Relax*, back in the 1930s. The technique involves tensing and untensing different muscle groups in the body. Once the tension is given up, the muscles naturally relax. Here is a procedure for deep muscle relaxation that can help you learn how to relax. The technique can be shortened for use on the court.

Start by practicing this series of movements:

1. *Right and left hand and forearm:* Make very tight fists and then let them go.
2. *Right and left upper arms:* Press your elbows down into the armrest of the chair or into the bed. While pressing down, move your upper arms toward your rib cage. Then release all the way.
3. *Forehead:* Raise your eyebrows as high as you can, then release. (If this movement does not produce tension, try making a deep frown.)
4. *Middle face:* With your eyelids shut tightly, wrinkle your nose, then release.
5. *Jaws:* While pressing your tongue to the roof of your mouth, clench your teeth tightly, then release.
6. *Neck:* Pull your chin down to your chest, and at the same time pull your head back with the muscles at the rear of your neck, then release.

7. *Shoulders and upper back:* Shrug your shoulders as if you were trying to touch your ears, then release.

8. *Stomach:* Suck your stomach in while forcing it downward. Make it hard, as if you expected someone to hit you with a fist, then let it go slack.

9. *Thighs:* Tense the muscles in your thighs, then release.

10. *Calves:* Bend your feet upward toward your shins as if you were trying to touch your shins with your toes, then release.

When you are familiar with how each movement feels, you are ready to begin using progressive relaxation.

• Find a quiet room where you will not be disturbed or distracted. Keep the lights dim.

• Choose a comfortable bed, couch, or overstuffed recliner. All parts of your body must be supported without strain; if you have to work to stay in place, you will not be able to relax completely.

• Wear loose-fitting clothing. Remove any tight clothes or undergarments, as well as shoes, eyeglasses, and contact lenses.

• Start by making yourself as comfortable as possible.

• Settle back until you feel completely supported.

• Take a deep breath. Fill your lungs with air and hold your breath for 5 seconds.

• Release your breath and let yourself begin to relax, letting go of the tension in your body.

• Tense the muscles of your hands and forearms. Hold that tension for 5 to 7 seconds. Study the feelings; be aware of what this tension feels like.

• Relax. Release the tension immediately and completely, not gradually. Feel the relaxation spread into your arms and hands. Study it; be aware of the difference between relaxation and tension. Enjoy the pleasant sensation for 20 to 30 seconds.

• Repeat the procedure on the upper arms: Tense the muscles and hold for 5 to 7 seconds (find a time length that feels right for you). Focus on the tension. Then release the muscles and concentrate on the feeling of relaxation for 20 to 30 seconds. Notice the difference between the two feelings. Enjoy the pleasant sensations as your muscles loosen and relax.

• Move on to the next muscle group and perform the recommended movement. Repeat it, and then move on to the next muscle group, and the next, and so on until you have completed all the movements twice for all the muscle groups.

• As you lie without moving, mentally explore each of the muscle groups you have relaxed. If you feel any remaining tension in any area simply repeat the tense-and-relax movement for that area. If you are free of tension, quietly enjoy your calm, peaceful feelings.

• End by imagining yourself in a calm, peaceful scene—it might be the green security of a quiet forest, or a sunlit beach with you alone and listening to the gentle ocean waves. Imagine yourself anywhere you feel safe and secure and at peace. Visualize the place in your mind and picture yourself there, completely at ease, rested and relaxed, untroubled by the events of the outside world. Enjoy this peaceful state for 10 minutes, or for as long as you like.

You may find it easier to record these instructions on tape, along with the proper timing cues. This frees you to concentrate on the movement without having to remember what to do next.

Progressive relaxation produces the most benefit when it is practiced twice a day. Once you have practiced it for a few days you will find yourself able to relax more easily and much more quickly. As with any skill, practice makes a great difference; but once it is learned, deep muscle relaxation is a most effective weapon against stress.

Tennis applications

Obviously, you can't lie down in the middle of the court to do deep breathing or deep muscle relaxation. If you practice these techniques on your own, however, you soon will reach a point where you can perform a shortened version on your feet. You will be able, for example, to tense your body briefly and then let go, triggering much of the relaxation you learned to attain through the full deep muscle relaxation exercise. You also will be able to take one deep breath, let it out slowly, and center yourself to maintain this sense of peace and balance. Combine these techniques—muscle tensing and relaxing, followed by a deep breath—and you have a powerful relaxation tool to use any time you wish.

In the Three R's system, you always relax as part of your Reset routine, even when you want to rev up as well. You also can relax during the Review phase to help clear your mind. The concept is to use the time between points to build in relaxation as an intervening event between two points of active play. This lets you play fresh, without residual tension from a previous point interfering with what you need to do for the current one.

HUMOR

Laughter can play a role in reducing stress, bringing a general feeling of well-being to the body and helping the healing process. For a vivid description of this process, see Norman Cousins' *Anatomy of an Illness*. In addition to the relaxing effects of laughter, humor allows you as a tennis player to break the tension, and to view the match from a different perspective. This can be a huge boost to your confidence—and often can be used to help you get out of a rut of bad play and lift you to a new level of performance.

How can you cultivate humor to enhance your tennis? Start by knowing that any opportunity you have to laugh, whether through books, comics, movies, plays, or simply joking around with your friends, is a way of practicing the art of letting humor and laughter be a part of your life and consequently your game. The transfer from everyday life to the tennis court will be more natural if you allow yourself to laugh at other aspects of living as they occur.

Beyond this, two other guidelines will help you make good use of humor in your tennis. First, steer clear of humor that makes fun of your opponent, or that occurs at someone else's expense. Instead, look for the humor in your own behavior and your own performance as a way of distancing yourself from mistakes. When making fun of your own mistakes, you Release the negative energy and clear the way for a correction on the next point.

Think of humor as a way to disengage from what just happened. All good humor, whether stand-up comedy, the written word, or jokes among friends, is grounded in taking a perspective or a view of a problem that is different from the one that everyone else is taking at the time. The punch line to a joke works because it is unexpected and surprises us. And it feels good to laugh! Look for opportunities to make jokes about your own play and lighten your own load.

MEDITATION

Depending upon your own philosophy of life and religious orientation, meditation might already be a part of your daily living. For some people, meditation takes the form of focused prayer to a higher power, and for others it involves establishing a quiet and relaxed state, and, with eyes closed, either thinking about nothing at all or focusing upon a particular word or concept. Meditation has a great deal in common with imagery, self-talk, and relaxation, but we list it as a separate tool because its focus goes beyond each of these alone, and even beyond the three of them taken together. Meditation is a process through which an athlete can reserve energy and focus not only on the event about to occur, but on life itself.

You can find volumes written on meditation, usually from the point of view of a particular religious tradition. Herbert Benson's *The Relaxation Response* draws together many of the common elements and adapts them for secular as well as religious use. As a basic outline, most systems of meditation involve steps like these:

1. *Regular practice:* Find a time each day when you choose to meditate (whether morning, during the day, or evening), and faithfully adhere to this special time away from the routine of your day.

2. *Turn attention away from events:* You can do this by closing your eyes, but the underlying concept is to get away from the sounds of radio and television, as well as interaction with other people, and focus instead on something that is seemingly unrelated to your regular activities.

3. *Focus on a higher power or special word.* Depending upon your religious tradition, you may experience the presence of God or a higher power, opening your mind and heart to influence, instruction, and support. Some will encourage this process through the repetition of a word to bring mental and spiritual focus.

4. *Relaxed deep breathing.* Slowing one's breathing slows the heart rate, and is another way to disengage from regular activities. Practiced in combination with the preceding techniques, the meditation experience is enhanced through the regulation of breathing to bring relaxation.

SUMMARY

None of these techniques is unique to sport psychology. Indeed, they have been borrowed from many other traditions in the behavioral sciences and the fields of religion and medicine. From the vantage point of sport psychology, they provide the necessary tools for enhancing performance. We draw on all of them in the Three R's Sport Psychology System. The system makes use of one or more of these tools in each of the three phases.

MARTINA HINGIS

Martina Hingis began playing tennis at the age of three and began playing tournaments at the age of five. In 1997, at age 16, she became the youngest player in Open Era play to win Wimbledon. She rounded out 1997 with nine singles tournament wins and 5 doubles wins, pushing her number of career singles titles to 11 and doubles titles to 8. The year 1997 was also notable because at the Australian Open, Martina won her first career Grand Slam singles title since turning professional at 14, becoming the youngest Grand Slam winner in Open Era play.

At this point in her career, Hingis is known for a practically flawless game whether it be backhands, forehands, volleys, or serves. She uses solid Reviews and quickness to keep an upper hand against her opponents. Though clay is her favorite surface, she has shown a dominance on all surfaces.

Martina Hingis, named after Martina Navratilova, was born in Kosice, Slovakia, on September 30, 1980 (She and her family moved to Switzerland when she was seven). She comes from a family steeped in tennis. Hingis is coached by her mother, Melanie Monitor, and her father, Karol Hingis, manages and coaches a tennis club in Trubbach, Switzerland. In her spare time she enjoys skiing, soccer, basketball, and horseback riding. She is superstitious about walking on the tennis court lines.

Martina Hingis

CHAPTER 3

The First R: Release

Every tennis point ends in either a win or a loss: You win the point through an opponent's error or your own good play, or you lose the point through your own error or your opponent's good play. If that were all there is to it—a point won or lost—then there would be no need for a Release between points. But we all know it is more complicated than that. As a human being, you might have deep feelings about your win or loss on a given point. If you make an unforced error, especially on a big point, then you might be mad at yourself when the point is over, or you might feel discouraged, or you might wonder, "What in the world do I have to do to win a point!" The key question is: What you do with the negative thought, the negative feeling, the negative energy?

Answer: Release it!

WHY RELEASE?

Robert Trogolo recalls watching one of his players in the early round of the U.S. Pro Indoors. "My player was totally dominating his opponent. Having won the first set 6–2, he was up 4–2, and serving to go up 5–2 with a lead of 40–love in the game. He served the first ball up the middle for an ace. He thought for sure it was an ace, and so did the line judge, but the umpire overruled the call. My guy went nuts! He started shouting at the umpire. The umpire said he had only 5 seconds to serve his second serve, so he told the umpire where to go. The umpire then gave him a warning. The second serve was out, which resulted in a double fault. That one incident marked the turning point in the match. My player could not recover from the bad line call, and went on to lose the match. His opponent went on to win the tournament."

In terms of the Three R's, Trogolo's player—instead of releasing the negative energy from the bad line call—kept the thought in his mind. He could not get past it, so he couldn't focus on playing out the next crucial points. There was a Release ("My guy went nuts!"), but the Release did not work. It led to more bad behavior (shouting at the umpire), then a warning, a double fault, and the whole downhill slide.

In its simplest form, a Release is an expression of feelings and energy after a point is over. There are good Releases and bad Releases. Bad Releases are those that get you in more trouble than you are already in, leaving you feeling worse about your play or even getting socked with code violations. Good Releases are those that allow you to get rid of the negative energy—literally leave it behind, so you can move on.

STARTING YOUR RELEASE

Based on your own experience, what's bad about the Releases on this list?

- Hitting a ball over the fence.
- Using loud profanity.
- Telling yourself, "You are so bad. I can't believe what a sorry excuse for a player you are! You are stupid!"
- Engaging in verbal combat with your opponent, perhaps resulting in a fistfight.

Let's take a closer look.

- *Hitting a ball over a fence, or into the stands.* If you break the rule about equipment abuse, you get a code violation and lose a point. Even worse, you might injure somebody. Remember when Jimmy Connors hit a ball into the stand and hit a spectator? Clearly, that kind of Release only makes things worse.

- *Profanity.* Another code violation. Even worse, by going over the edge with profane language, you demonstrate to yourself and to your opponent that you are out of control. And all the while, your opponent is feeding off your misfortune.

- *Negative talk.* When you call yourself "bad" or "stupid," you compound the situation. Bad play is one part of the problem; labeling yourself as bad and stupid becomes a second problem. You may start to live up to your own prophecy—and play even worse! (Tennis is tough enough without your adding to it by getting down on yourself!)

• *Verbal combat.* Anything that distracts you from the task at hand (executing your shots, working your game plan) carries the risk of throwing you way off course.

TAKING THE NEXT STEP

A better Release is one that gets rid of the energy, but lets you hold your head high, maintain your integrity, and look strong to your opponent. The last bit is an important part of the game of tennis. After all, you are the only real support you have out there, and the image you project to your opponent is one that may make or break your game. If you look strong, you are more intimidating than if you look like you are falling apart. If you look like you are falling apart, your opponent gets pumped up and moves in for the kill.

What if, instead of letting your energy out in a way that demeans you, you let it out in a way that says, "I don't like what just happened, but I can deal with it! Watch me get better!" Some of the top players do this with humor, antics, or phrases that let them blow off steam without harming their games. For example:

• *You dump a volley into the net.* Instead of screaming or turning away with slumped shoulders and a dejected look, you immediately imitate the shot you wish you had hit, thereby locking in the positive. You turn an error into an improved imaginary shot, ready for the next one to be even better when the ball is in play. If you want to see how this is done, watch Boris Becker or Michael Chang. We once saw Becker hit a shot into the net, and immediately take a ball from his pocket, drop it as if he were in a practice session, and hit the stroke smoothly, with good net clearance and heavy topspin, right back to the ball boy in the corner. He wasn't bashing the ball in anger, he just corrected the shot that he missed. Michael Chang is another player who will do this. We have seen him hit an imaginary shot three or four times between points to make sure he has a clear picture of what the proper shot feels like, the shot he just missed or the one he wants to handle correctly the next time he gets a chance.

• *You play a bad shot.* Instead of saying, "You're so stupid," you say, "I can't believe that!" Emphasize that you are upset with

that one stroke, not your whole life! By criticizing this one behavior, you allow for the idea that your play can improve, even though that particular point or shot was bad.

• *Your opponent calls the ball out when you thought it was in.* You do what Chris Evert used to do. Instead of an angry protest, you glare at the spot where the ball hit. Without speaking a word, you "question the call" with a glare.

• *You make an unforced error.* Instead of berating yourself, you look to the heavens and spread your arms wide, as if to say, "Why me, Lord?"

In these examples, you are letting your feelings out (Releasing the energy, letting go of the point), and you are letting them out without throwing yourself into an emotional ditch.

Peak performers in tennis have perfected a variety of Releases so that they always have several options, no matter what happens on the court. Sometimes only the player knows what the Release is, or even that there's been one. Things are going well in the match, nothing bad has happened yet, and after a point, the player simply thinks to himself, "All right, keep it up." This thought releases energy after the point is over.

On another occasion, a player has come back after being down 0–40, and a fist pump coupled with the words "Come on!" or some other physical Release keeps the momentum going. At another time, when things are going badly, a player may use humor to let out the negative so that it does not spill forward and paint the next point. We have seen Jimmy Connors, after a string of bad shots, walk over and hand his racket to someone in the stands as if to say, "Surely you can play better than I can. Come on and take over for me." We recall seeing Andre Agassi give his racket to a ball girl, and let her play a whole point.

Let us summarize what we have said so far about good Releases:

1. The amount of Release will vary, depending on where you are in the match. In the early going, it may seem as if you don't have many feelings to Release. You may be playing ordinary points, and as soon as one is over, you are ready to move on to the next one. As you get more into the match, however, there will be more to feel good or bad about. You can feel good about your own play, or the lead you are building. You can feel bad about the mistakes you are making, or the way you can't seem to get on track, or your opponent's good play. By engaging in some acceptable expression after the point is over, you are simply allowing yourself to be a human being and to feel good or bad after a point.

2. At the heart of the Release phase is a letting go of the previous point, so you can go on to the next one. It might sound trivial, but unless you let go of what just happened, you will have a hard time grabbing the new opportunity that the next point presents. At a later stage in the Three R's, we will help you Review what has happened and prepare for making an adjustment in the next point. It will be easier to do this if you have let go of the previous point. It's almost like climbing a ladder. You can't put your hand on the next rung until you let go of the one below it.

3. The Release can be a very private matter. You may simply say something under your breath, or think a thought that fulfills all of the requirements of a good Release. It need not be a public display.

4. Humor can be a great Release. The ability to find humor in a situation requires having a perspective on what is going on. Humor can lead to laughter, which can lead to relaxation, which

will help your tennis. Look for opportunities to laugh at your-self, and you will be on your way to a Release that you can use to your advantage.

5. Be creative in fashioning constructive Releases. Question-ing a line call is a form of Release. If your opponent (or a line judge) makes a call you don't like, the way you glare at the ball mark or raise a question ("Are you sure?") or engage in any dis-cussion is all a matter of Release. The important part is to Re-lease your feelings and views in a way that is assertive but does not throw off your own concentration. A good Release might

include body language, talking out loud, talking to yourself, or all three. For example, body language might include throwing your arms up in the air, or imitating the shot you missed to correct it. Similarly, you speak or groan out loud as another form of Release. And finally, by talking to yourself (*self-talk,* psychologists call it, the internal patter no one else can hear), you also are engaging in a Release. Indeed, you can say things to yourself that others should not hear—if they did it might get you in more trouble.

6. Emphasize the positive. One of our junior players put it this way: "Negative releases don't help me. They just bring me down." If you let out a string of negative words after a bad point, you run the danger of starting a downward spiral. On the other hand, if you make fun of what just happened with humor, or immediately imitate the shot you wish you had played, you get the double benefit of letting the feelings out and lifting the bad moment to a higher, more positive plane. After all, the next thing you want to do is the positive, so start right now by imitating it.

SAMPLE RELEASES

At the end of this chapter we will help you develop your own preferred Releases. You may want to draw from some of these tested versions.

"Fixing" the Shot

One of the most powerful things you can do following a shot that you have missed is to imitate the shot and correct the mistake you have just made, while at the same time giving yourself a verbal instruction.

It goes like this. Suppose you opened up too quickly on your backhand and sprayed the ball wide. Instead of whatever you might ordinarily do, tell yourself, "Not like that. Like this!" At the same time, make an appropriate turn and step in to hit an imaginary ball, this time keeping your shoulders properly "closed" until the last moment.

What you are doing is correcting the error you just made. This becomes a tremendously powerful Release because it takes the negative energy and puts it into a corrective mode. You have recognized what you have done wrong, and you are now telling yourself what to do, and modeling and demonstrating how to do it right. It lets your last memory of the failed shot be the correction, which will help you on the next point. Also, it presents a fairly intimidating image to an opponent. An opponent will begin to think: "What do I have to do to beat you? You correct mistakes as you make them. I can't seem to break you down."

New Words

Nothing can be so vexing to a player (or coach, or family member) as the profanity and other words that seem to spew forth during tough times on the court. Some players find it almost impossible to stop saying these words. It is as if a button gets pushed and there seems to be no way to stop what will happen next. The problem is understandable—competitive tennis is a form of combat, and it makes sense that someone who is playing hard and aggressively to win also will be verbally combative between points—combative with himself or herself, and with an opponent. So what can you do to channel aggressive energy away from words that bring on code violations and fines, and turn it in a more constructive direction?

The Three R's approach is to define alternative words well ahead of time, and practice these instead of the words that draw violations. If you are a player who needs to "let it out," then treat this as one of your strengths—but redefine what letting it out will mean in your case. Instead of swear words, select and practice saying words to take their place. Before you say this will not work for you, remember that profane people throughout history have used the same technique to keep themselves out of trouble. Words like gosh and darn are simply variations on words that people have found unacceptable in social situations. In formulating your words, you might draw on the following approaches that have worked for other players:

1. *Drop all the consonants.* Don't say a word at all, just give a loud groan or other utterance. "Aaah!" You can't do this too loudly or you will disrupt play on the other courts, but it could be a way to express your pain without saying a real word. (As a variation, pick up a towel and yell into it.)

2. *Talk about behavior only.* Talk about what you just did instead of saying negative things about yourself, the world, the deities, and the cosmos. For example: "I can't believe this." "*That* was a terrible shot." "You better improve that." All these statements focus on the behavior, as opposed to you as a person—or anyone else. If I tell myself that I can't play, or that I am stupid, then I begin to adjust my game to this characterization. On the other hand, if I say something more balanced about what just

happened ("A bad line call, yes, but you can come back, now let's get going, let's do it!"), then I have turned adversity into a challenge, and a negative becomes a positive.

3. *Use substitute words.* If you know words from other languages (not swear words), that have a good sound and feel for you, try saying these. One student with two years of high school German used to enjoy saying *"Ausgezeichnet!"* and *"Ach Du meiner güte."* The gutturals allow a strong expression of feeling, but the words actually translate into "Excellent" and "Oh, my goodness!"— though you certainly would not know that to hear them on the court (unless you speak German). Try developing your own substitute word ("Great!" "Fantastic!") to use instead of profanity. The more you use it, the more likely you are to say it under stress, when you really need it. See table 3.1.

Table 3.1 Releases

Constructive	Destructive
Corrective comments: "Stay down! Watch the ball!"	No comment—allowing bad play to sink in and get worse.
Pump up words: "Come on!" "Yes!" "That's it!"	No words (or thoughts) of encouragement.
Pump up action—pump fist, slap leg.	No action—internal tension builds.
Private thoughts: "You're doing great! Keep it up!"	Private thoughts: "You can't do it."
Compliment opponent: "Too good!""Great shot!" Applaud with racket.	Scowl in disbelief or make disparaging remark to opponent.
Use humor after an error.	Live with the pain.
Imitate the good shot to override the bad one in your memory.	Let the bad shot stay in your mind and become the last thought before the next point.

STOP THE RELEASE

The flow of the Three R's system requires an end point for each phase: Release, Review, and Reset. The end point of Reset is obvious: Serving or returning serve marks the clear end of between-point activity, and the beginning of playing out the point.

Ending the Release and Review phases, however, requires a separate action on your part. Tennis players are vulnerable off the task—between points, between matches—because it is so easy to fall into endless negative Releases or obsessively ruminating Reviews. If the feelings of the Release or the mental activity of the Review do not end, then they spill over into the next point. We sometimes refer to this as *painting* the next point. Think of your own experience, or consider some of the great players you have observed. It is easy to remember times where stopping the Release soon enough would have kept someone out of serious trouble—code violations, even disqualification. The trick is to get the satisfaction of a solid Release as described in this chapter, then to move on to the Review, which is also critical to improving performance on the next point.

The solution is to STOP Release behavior with a preplanned word, and, as will be discussed in chapter 4, to STOP Review behavior in the same way. By giving yourself the simple verbal instruction, "STOP," you can end whatever you are doing, at least for that moment. In the case of the Three R's, once you end the Release behavior, you can move easily to Review.

Practice the STOP technique with a friend. Begin counting from 1 to 20, and let your friend interrupt you by shouting "STOP!" at some point. Notice how this gets you to stop counting. The next number simply doesn't get spoken. If you can follow this simple step, then you will have learned the STOP technique.

The next step is to turn your attention away from what just occurred (in this case, counting from 1 to 20), and turn to something else. Try having your friend tell you to begin saying the alphabet immediately after the STOP. For example:

You: "1, 2, 3, 4, 5—"

Your friend: "STOP! Now, start saying your ABCs."

You: "A, B, C, D, E, F, G . . ."

In this simple sequence, you will notice that you are able to go immediately from one activity (counting) to another activity (saying your ABCs), with one simple instruction, STOP. This is just what you do in the Three R's when you move from the Release phase to the Review phase. After you finish your Release, you say to yourself (so no one else can hear): "STOP." Then give yourself some cue sequence you've worked out in advance and move smoothly into the Review phase.

EXERCISES TO HELP YOU RELEASE

Exercise 1

Evaluate your own current Release behavior by answering the following questions and rating your responses as follows:

Rarely = 1
Some of the time = 2
Most of the time = 3
All or almost all of the time = 4

_____a. Profanity is a part of my between-point behavior.

_____ b. I get code violations from outbursts.

_____ c. I use humor to deal with adversity.

_____ d. I attack my opponent verbally.

_____ e. I throw my racket, hit the ball against the screen, or engage in other forms of equipment abuse.

_____ f. I get so mad that sometimes I cannot cool down before I play the next point.

_____ g. My self-talk is quite negative.

_____ h. I sometimes imitate the shot I missed in order to "fix" it before the next point.

Exercise 1, (continued)

_____ i. I talk out on the court, but my words do not draw code violations.

_____ j. I sulk after a bad shot, keeping my feelings inside.

A. Scoring Instructions: Record the score for each item in the appropriate box.

Strengths	Deficits	
c. _____	a. _____	f. _____
h. _____	b. _____	g. _____
i. _____	d. _____	j. _____
	e. _____	

B. Strengths: Scores of 3 or 4 on items c, h, and i indicate that you are
already incorporating constructive releases into your between-point
behavior.

C. Deficits: Scores of 2, 3, or 4 on items a, b, d, e, f, g, and j indicate that
you are vulnerable to breakdowns in the Release phase, which could have
a negative effect on how you play the next point.

Exercise 2

One way to improve your Releases is to make a list of the Releases
that fit your personality and that you would like to incorporate into
your game. You should give this list the same attention you would
give to selecting a racket, or to picturing the kind of serve or forehand
you wish to develop. Use the following checklist to identify elements
of your own customized Release. (Check as many items as apply to
your game.)

Exercise 2, (continued)

I Will:	I Will Avoid:
☐ Make corrective comments (such as "Stay down!").	☐ Global negatives ("You're so bad," "You stink").
☐ Say "Come on," "Yes," "That's it" (after doing well on big point).	☐ Profanity.
	☐ Racket, ball, people abuse.
☐ Use fist pump.	☐ Other (list):
☐ Use humor after an error.	_____
☐ Imitate the good shot to correct the bad one.	_____
☐ Do all of this in a quiet way.	_____
☐ Compliment my opponent ("Too good," "Great shot," applaud with racket).	
☐ Other (list):	
_____	
_____	
_____	

STOP

Looking at the items you have checked, and in light of your history with Releases, write a summary of what you want to include in your Release phase.

_____

_____

_____

_____

Exercise 3

Practice your own Release each time you are on the court (whether playing a match or in a practice game). Have a friend code your Releases from a live match or from a videotape using the coding sheet in chapter 7.

STEFAN EDBERG

Stefan Edberg won his first junior Grand Slam singles title by triumphing over the field at the U.S. Open in 1983. In 1990 and again in 1991, Edberg was placed first in the year-end rankings. By the end of 1996, the right-hander had racked up 41 career singles titles and 18 doubles titles, winning tournaments on all surfaces: carpet, clay court, grass court, and hard court. He has a record of 51 consecutive Grand Slam appearances, the all-time best record in the history of Grand Slam tennis. He also shares the distinction with John McEnroe of being the only players to be ranked No. 1 in both singles and doubles play.

Where Muster's and Chang's strength is speed and counterattack, Edberg's chief strength is his ability to maintain a focused attack through strong serves and volleys. During play, Edberg maintains a cool demeanor with subdued Releases. He follows through with solid Reviews that help him maintain his concentration.

Stefan Edberg was born on January 19, 1966, in Västervik, Sweden. He is married to Annette Olson and they have two children, Emilie Victoria Edberg and Christoffer Edberg. When he announced his retirement at the close of 1996, he was among only four players in the modern era to have played more than 1,000 matches. He resides in London.

© Tommy Hindley

Stefan Edberg

CHAPTER 4

The Second R: Review

The second R in the Three R's system is the "Review". It gives you a chance to either affirm your game plan (If it's working, keep it up!) or to find some way to get your game on track. We'll show you how to Review in this chapter—but first let's take a closer look at the rationale behind it.

WHY REVIEW?

Your Review lets you evaluate where you are, and make any adjustments necessary to improve your situation. If the game is going well, you won't want to change a thing. Remember the old adage, "If it ain't broke, don't fix it." This applies to your game plan. If you're doing something right (for example, strong slice service return to keep the ball low and make it harder for your opponent to volley), then during your Review you will tell yourself, "Stay with it, watch the ball, make a good return."

Or you may discover that you have been deserting your game plan, and you need to remind yourself to get back to it. For example, if you planned to chip and charge to get in to the net but forgot to do it, the Review is your time to make this adjustment.

Another objective of the Review might be to change your game plan. Your opponent is presenting you with new problems or new opportunities that you had not anticipated. No coach can help you now. You evaluate the situation and tell yourself what adjustment to make on the next point.

STARTING YOUR REVIEW

One of the simplest things you can do to start your Review is turn away from the net and your opponent, switch your racket to your nonplaying hand, and walk toward the back court, perhaps looking at the strings as you go. The purpose of this little maneuver is

ANCHOR YOUR REVIEW

You will notice that in the Three R's system we rely on behavioral cues to make the system work. The reason for this is that in the heat of a match, it is hard to think about what you should be doing between points. You want to develop good habits that trigger the appropriate phases of the Three R's: Release, Review, and Reset. Switching your racket to your other hand and turning away from the net is an effective cue to begin the Review. Some psychologists would view this as a way to *anchor* the Review. We have known some players who wear a rubber band on their wrists, and snap it between points to remind themselves to get in the game, stay with the game plan, or whatever they have decided they most need to remember. Whatever method you use, choose a simple behavioral step that will start the Review for you.

to prompt you to start your Review. It should be so ingrained that as soon as the racket hits your nonplaying hand, you begin the Review phase. On a videotape of your between-point activity, you should be able to see when you started your Review.

Here's where habit is your friend. Develop a pattern of movement that begins the Review, and file it in the same part of your brain that enables you to put on your shoes, brush your teeth, and perform other voluntary actions without having to think about them.

By starting the Review this way you can condition yourself to do a Review even when big-time distractions come your way (see the "Anchor Your Review" box).

TAKING THE NEXT STEP

Once you have made the behavioral prompt to start Reviewing, what should you think about? There are two good options: What you can learn from what just happened (past), and what you can do next (future).

Suppose you are making a lot of unforced errors. Say you have been working the point, keeping the ball deep and creating short balls, but then you hit the short ball long or wide. During the Review, you will think about *why* this is happening. Perhaps you are running through the shot instead of getting set before you knock off the hard-earned short ball for a winner. Maybe you are so excited at finally having a chance to end the point that you take your eye off the ball. You are thinking ahead to the new score with you in the lead, so much so that you miss the shot. During the Review phase, you think about it in just this way.

Try asking yourself the standard "coach questions," the ones your own coach might ask you if he could:

"What just happened?"

"Why did I win the point?"

"Why did I lose the point?"

"Am I doing my game plan?"

"Am I playing to my opponent's weakness?"

"What do I need to do next?"

Here is the payoff for asking these Review questions: You learn from your mistakes (and your good points, too), and get stronger and smarter with each point. A good Review lets you

Table 4.1   Make Your Reviews Work

Do	Don't
Use specific behavior (such as switching racket to non-playing hand) to start Review.	Skip the behavioral step.
Relax with a deep breath in and out as you begin the Review.	Pace or walk to the ball in an agitated manner.
Walk confidently (shoulders back, head up).	Let racket hang from your playing hand, shoulders droop, and allow negative feelings show in your nonverbal behavior.
Look at strings, ground, or some other focal point to think.	Distract yourself by looking at others on the sideline (such as your coach, friends, or parents).
Ask the "coach question": • What just happened? • Why did I win the point? • Why did I lose the point? • Am I doing my game plan? • Am I playing my opponent's weakness? • What do I need to do next?	Neglect to ask these questions when it was part of your Review plan to do so.
Call Play 1, Play 2, Play 3 (see page 61).	Forget to Review your game plan.
Consider code words to bring focus to the Review (such as "Watch the ball!""Be strong!" "Play the ball!" or "Get in!")	Talk to yourself at length, without focus.

build on your success and correct for your weakness then and there on the spot. This makes you a strong competitor. You even turn the bad stuff to your advantage. Table 4.1 offers Review tips in a "Do's and Don'ts" format. The exercises at the end of the chapter also will help you create a customized Review, one that fits your game. Remember, too, that sometimes the Review will be brief, and at other times it may take a bit longer. The key is to make Review such a habit that you do it every time.

Review to Deal With Distractions

You have just lost a point, and you know it was because of poor concentration. To make matters worse, you allowed yourself to get distracted by an airplane noise—or by someone on the sidelines, or a stray thought about what a friend, parent, or coach might be thinking of your play. You feel bad enough about having lost the point, but these other distracting thoughts make matters worse. What do you do?

Start by allowing yourself to have the thought, perhaps even exaggerating it. Suppose, for example, that instead of watching the ball, you were watching someone in the crowd. As soon as you notice what you did, say to yourself so others cannot hear: "There you go, looking at that hat instead of at the ball!"

Or suppose you thought about what your coach would think of your play, instead of watching the ball. Then say to yourself: "Can you believe this, here I am thinking what my coach thinks instead of getting down to business!" Doing this lets you bring the thought into consciousness instead of allowing it to stay buried somewhere in your thoughts and feelings.

To underline what your mind is doing to you, you also can think to yourself, "That's interesting!" or "Look at that thought!" to punctuate what you have just discovered. For example, "Look at what I just did: Watched somebody in the crowd instead of the ball! That's interesting!"

On first glance, noticing that you were distracted may seem like a strange thing to do. The point is that you have to expose the distracting thought before you can replace it with something more appropriate. This is a concept you might apply to any business or life problem. Expose the problem with words: "I'm afraid to make that speech," or "I can't believe I just said something that stupid." Once your fear or frustration has been exposed, you will be in a position to move past it and take constructive action to correct the error.

Next, plan what you want to do in the next point. Think back to the objectives of the Review. Do you need to watch the ball better, or move your feet, or simply execute your shots by following through better? Do you want to recover your game plan—that is, go back to something that you planned on doing that you have forgotten to do? Pay close attention to staying with something that is already working. Many players, because they have a weak Review, will desert a game plan that is working. If it is working, stay with it. Remember what Darrell Royal, the famous football coach, said about a winning game plan: "Dance with the one who brung you!"

SAMPLE REVIEW

Here are some sample Review instructions that might be appropriate during the middle phase of the Three R's:

- *"Work her backhand!"* Sue made an amazing discovery. She found her opponent had a weak backhand during the warmup, and the first two games confirmed it. During the Review, Sue decided to work the point to get her opponent wide in the deuce court, and then force her to run to hit a backhand. During the Review, she thought this to herself, and pictured herself doing it on the next point.

- *"Get in!"* Tom got burned during long baseline rallies during the first two games of the first set. As he got ready to return serve in game three, he realized that he had gotten to the net only once. His coach had told him to chip and charge against this guy, but Tom had not been doing it. He decided to chip and charge on the very next point.

- *"Be aggressive!"* Blanche found herself falling into her opponent's game plan by staying back and simply returning whatever came to her. She had made a commitment to be aggressive against her opponent, work the point, and look for a short ball to attack, but realized she had not been doing it. During the Review she discovered this error, and said to herself: "Be aggressive."

• *"Block it out!"* Natasha was really thrown off by the airplane noise, and by the cheers that went up every time she lost a point. Natasha knew that she needed to block this out if she were to play well. She noticed that she was distracted, and thought to herself: "Can you believe this? Here I am thinking about the airplanes and the fans, and not watching the ball. I've got to stop that. Just watch the ball, and play the point. If I do that, I know I'll win!"

In each of these examples, the player is simply noticing what is happening on the court (or, more precisely, what has happened in the past, as well as what is happening right now), Reviewing the situation in terms of his or her knowledge of the game, and making a plan to do something constructive on the next ball.

Check Your Game Plan

As a tennis player, you can learn from other sports by creating a simple, easily remembered game plan with code numbers to bring focus to the Review phase of the Three R's system. For example, in basketball, football, and other sports, players call out plays that have numbers or names known to everyone on the team. A single number can tell all 11 players on a football team what their assignments are. Tennis players, on the other hand, often find themselves simply playing a match with no way to remember what their game plan is. If your memory goes blank, try one of these three standard tennis game plans, which are described in more detail in chapter 7.

Play 1 is the most aggressive: Serve and volley, or come in on the very next ball when you are returning. Play 1 says: "I am coming in to the net no matter what; after a serve, I'll run, do a split step, hit the volley, and close; I may have to hit an overhead, but I am going to win or lose the point at the net."

Play 2 says: "I will work the point from the baseline, but the very first time I get a short ball, I am coming in. I will knock off the short ball, then close for a volley or, if necessary, be ready to hit an overhead to win the point."

Play 3 is a standard baseline game: "I will hit good solid ground strokes from the baseline, work the point, and win with my precision, consistency, and power from the baseline."

As a part of your Review (looking back at what happened, and remembering your game plan) you can decide between points which play to use on the next point. For example, you can say to yourself, "Play 1," and this will tell you that you are going to serve and volley on the next point. "Play 2" would mean that you are going to work the point, but come in on a short ball.

Trogolo's coaching of Michael Chang in a match against Stefan Edberg illustrates the use of both game plan and code words during the Review phase. In the week prior to the match, Edberg had beaten Chang 6–1, 6–0. Michael had stayed back on everything, and Edberg came in on everything. The plan this time was for Michael to be more aggressive on the returns by hitting down the line. Also, on second serves his plan was to take the ball early and come in behind it, taking the net away from Edberg. The plan worked; in the first set Chang broke Edberg three times. The plan also required Chang to hold serve, and to mix up serves by coming in on some and staying back on others. The successful game plan included a combination of Play 1 and Play 2, and Chang won the match in straight sets.

Use Code Words

Keep it simple during the Review by using a code word to tell you what to do next. Tennis players and other athletes are noted for having short phrases to tell them what to do. We once saw Monica Seles in a match against Steffi Graf, and at the changeover Monica looked at her strings and shouted over and over: "Break her! You can break her! Come on!" One player went back to her room during a rain delay and put little adhesive notes all over the wall that each contained only one word: "Hold" or "Break." Very simple.

Other code words are: "Watch the ball!" "Play the ball!" "Get in!" "Be strong!" "Go for it!" Or you can use the code words for your game plan: Play 1, Play 2, or Play 3.

Always wrap up your Review phase with a code word about what you are going to do next.

STOP THE REVIEW

The STOP is your best friend when it comes to putting an end to too much thinking. One of Trogolo's players used to say "Stop!" to keep negative thinking about his doubles partner's bad play from spilling over into the next point. Even though they had talked things over before the match and were trying to communicate better on court, there was only so much this player could do. At a certain point, the only appropriate thing to do was to STOP all thinking, move on to Reset, and get ready for the next point. The STOP technique saved the day for this player. Say the word "Stop!" to yourself after you have finished the Review. This will be your cue to stop thinking and begin a preplanned and practical set of relaxing and focusing behaviors—your Reset routine—before serving or returning.

As described in chapter 2, you can learn the STOP technique by starting any behavioral sequence such as counting and having a friend yell "Stop!" at any point. From that point on, the word will mean that it is time to stop whatever you are doing and move on to the next phase which, in this case, is your Reset routine.

EXERCISES TO HELP YOU REVIEW

Exercise 1

Answer these questions: To what extent have you been one to think too much—or too little—while on the court between points? Can you identify matches in which you were hurt because your Review between points wasn't sufficiently focused?

Exercise 2

Create your own Review by checking items from the list in this exercise. Then write your own summary Review in the lines that follow. For example: "After saying STOP (following Release) I will immediately switch racket hands, look at my strings, and walk as I go over the situation. Relaxing as I walk, I will ask myself the "coach questions" and check my game plan. Then I will call either Play 1, Play 2, or Play 3 before beginning my Reset routine."

Exercise 2, (continued)

I Will:	I Will Avoid:
☐ Switch racket to nonplaying hand to start Review.	☐ Skipping the Review.
☐ Walk confidently (shoulders back, head up).	☐ Looking just at the bad.
☐ Look at my strings as I think.	☐ Forgetting my game plan.
☐ Ask the "coach questions."	☐ Looking at coach (parents) for help.
☐ What just happened?	☐ Other (list):
☐ Why did I win the point?	_____
☐ Why did I lose the point?	_____
☐ Am I doing my game plan?	_____
☐ Am I playing my opponent's weakness?	
☐ What do I need to do next?	
☐ Call "Play 1," "Play 2," or "Play 3."	
☐ Say my code words (such as "Watch the ball," "Be strong," "Play the ball," "Get in!").	
☐ Relax with deep breathing.	
☐ Other (list):	
_____	
_____	
_____	

Looking at the items you have checked, write down a summary of what would be an ideal Review for you between points.

_____

_____

_____

Exercise 3

Practice your own Review, and ask a friend to code your Review behavior live or on videotape using the Coding Manual in chapter 7.

Exercise 4

Watch other players (live or on TV) to see if you can spot good and poor Reviews. For example, can you tell when taking too little time for the Review leads to rushed play and unforced errors (especially after things have gone badly for a point or two)?

BILLIE JEAN KING

What kind of mental toughness does it take to beat Bobby Riggs in the "Battle of the Sexes" before a worldwide audience? Those who watched that match recall that Riggs had previously defeated Margaret Court in another battle of the sexes, and that Riggs went through all sorts of distracting maneuvers, even presenting Margaret with a bouquet of roses just as the match started. Billie Jean told the world that she would not let herself get distracted, and she proved it.

Billie Jean King was the first woman to be given the title "Sportsperson of the Year" by *Sports Illustrated* in 1972, and in 1973 she was named "Female Athlete of the Year." In 1962, when she was 18, King upset Margaret Smith Court, the best woman player, at Wimbledon. In 1967 King was the first woman since 1939 to have won the triple crown in singles, doubles, and mixed doubles in both the British and American championships. By 1968 she had captured Wimbledon three times and would go on to win it three more times before retiring. In all, she won 71 career tournaments, 39 Grand Slam singles titles, and 27 Grand Slam doubles titles. King was the first woman athlete to win more than $100,000 in prize money in a single season.

King's outspoken support for better pay and treatment for women players, as well as her defeat of Bobby Riggs, were instrumental in improving the popularity of women's tennis. Known to be a fierce competitor, King employed an all-out attack on the court while maintaining a tight focus on her game plan with solid Reviews.

Billie Jean King (Moffit) was born on November 22, 1943, in Long Beach, California. After retiring, King became a coach and television analyst for the sport. She established the first successful women's professional tennis tour and founded tennis clinics for underprivileged children.

Billie Jean King

CHAPTER 5 The Third R: Reset Routine

Watch professional tennis players as they get ready to serve or return serve, and you'll notice patterns in their behavior. Some look at their opponent or glance unobtrusively at a spot on the court where they intend to hit the first serve. Others go through a specific ball bounce routine. Some take a deep breath and seem to draw a mental image of what they are going to do. (You'll see this in other sports as well. Watch basketball players shooting free throws, placekickers getting ready to kick field goals, or baseball players stepping into the batter's box.) Many players go through rituals, such as John McEnroe pulling on his shirt, or Ivan Lendel pulling on his eyelids in certain situations. Others will bounce on their toes before returning serve, then do a split step in preparation for hitting the ball.

WHY RESET?

Our analysis of these routines and rituals is that players use them to Reset themselves before the next point. Instead of being dragged down by some terrible thing that just happened (bad line call, noise from the stands, or feelings of impending doom when a weaker player manages to get ahead of them), these players do something to get themselves into a better frame of mind for the next point. You can start your computer working again when it gets itself tied in knots simply by pressing a button. Tennis (and life) is a bit more complicated, so it takes a more complex behavioral routine to Reset yourself when you need a fresh start.

STARTING YOUR RESET ROUTINE

Picture John McEnroe at his worst and best! No matter how dramatic his outbursts or how they threw his opponent off, when it came time to serve or return, there was never a player as good at putting what had just occurred behind him, completing specific behavioral routines, and bringing complete focus to the task at hand.

This chapter will give you a checklist for completing the third R, Reset, between points. We suggest that you use a regular routine for your Reset, so the power of conditioned habit will carry you through no matter what's happening in the game. You may have such a routine already—many players are fairly strong on this part of the game—without noticing that you're doing anything specific. Without the underlying concept, however, players commonly rush their normal routine under stressful circumstances, or skip it altogether. Just as bad, they might allow distractions to throw off their Reset routine, and keep them from using it to enhance concentration and focus when they need it most.

TAKING THE NEXT STEP

Think of the Reset as a best friend who helps you maintain (or regain) your composure as you prepare to put the ball in play. In no case do you want to let someone steal your Reset from you by interrupting the flow. As a matter of fact, if you're ever interrupted between points (a ball rolls onto the court, crowd noise gets unusually loud, or your opponent does something to throw you off), begin the Three R's all over again, from the top: Brief Release, brief Review of the situation, and then complete your Reset routine. We'll get back to ways to deal with interruptions later, but let's look at some basic Reset routines first.

SAMPLE RESET ROUTINE

You can develop a routine that is uniquely suited to your style of play. This means that your routine may be very different from that of other players, even though all players will draw from several standard components illustrated in table 5.1. Have a look at the table and the discussion of the components, and see which elements you would like to include in your Reset routine, and in what order.

Service

Here are some of the measures that we've found helpful when getting ready to serve.

• *Look to opposite court.* Before stepping to the line to serve, look at the opponent, or the other side of the court, indicating that you are in control of the situation, and about to put the ball in play.

Table 5.1   Reset Routine Components

When Serving	When Returning
Step to the line.	Step to the line.
Call score.	Check score.
Relax with a deep breath in and out; image a great serve to start the point.	Relax with a deep breath in and out; imagine your strong return (say, chip and charge).
Bounce the ball a set number of times.	Begin "fast feet."
Begin serve motion.	Move to the return.

Note. This is a basic relaxation-oriented Reset routine. You can add Rev Up elements by starting the process with a slap to your leg, saying "Come On!" to yourself, or going through some other motion to get yourself going as you step to the line. Note that you still want to relax midway through the Reset routine, so as to settle in at the new energy level and make sure you're ready to play your best.

• *Call the score.* Unless you have someone calling the score for you, you can step to the line and call the score (if returning, ask for the score to be called, if your opponent fails to do so).

• *Relax with a deep breath, and exhale.* Imagine putting the ball into play, and then bounce the ball. This sequence of behaviors can be ordered to suit your own style. The concept is to relax by taking a deep breath and exhaling (much as basketball players do before shooting free throws), conjure up an image of what you are about to do, and then bounce the ball any number of times that seems to suit you. Always use the same number of bounces—the number itself doesn't matter, but the repetition builds a sense of control at a nonverbal level and transfers to similar control when you actually serve.

• *Serve the ball.* At this point you begin your service motion, which has a behavioral routine of its own. Beginning from a start position (ball and racket held together), you bend your knees, moving the racket back and tossing the ball, and then uncoil your body and hit the ball with tremendous energy and power in precisely the direction that you have already imagined. The ball is now in play and you are off and running!

Return

Use any combination of the following as a part of your return routine.

• *Imagine your return.* Picture what you are going to do on the return. Imagine how you will watch the ball come off the opponent's racket, quickly make your move to return, and hit the ball well.

• *Relax.* Take a deep breath and let it out slowly. Shake loose any jitters before you step into the return area.

• *Look at opponent on other side of the court.* As with the service, looking at the opponent on the other side can be your way of controlling the situation and letting the person know that you are ready to return.

• *Step to the return area and begin footwork.* This may involve bouncing on your toes, swaying back and forth, or any other behavioral routine that allows you to prepare to return a good shot.

Variations: Relax or Rev Up

Players report that when they are "in the zone" of peak performance, they are able to effortlessly execute shots without a lot of thought. They are neither too relaxed nor too excited. While you cannot force yourself into the zone, you certainly can create conditions that make getting there possible. If you are too relaxed, you may need to pump yourself up. If you are too pumped up, you may need to relax yourself. You can do this by varying your Reset routine as either a *relax routine* or a *rev up routine.*

Use a relax routine if you are uptight, nervous, or too energized. The routines already described are relax routines. In these routines you take a deep breath, let it out slowly, collect yourself, then get ready to serve the ball or return.

If you have learned in your Review phase that you are too calm, underaroused, lethargic, or unmotivated, and you need to get going, then do a rev up routine. Add one or more of the following to your standard routine to rev you up:

- *Say "Come on!" or some other phrase.* Tell yourself to get going.
- *Slap your leg, as if to wake yourself up.* Or do something else to get your attention.
- *Use aggressive imagery about the next point.* Picture what you are going to be doing in a strong, positive way. Picture taking control of the entire point.

Here's more on how to make imagery a part of your (relax or rev up) Reset routine as you get ready to serve or return. Picture yourself about to play a classic tennis point. If you are going to play serve and volley and you have chosen Play 1, then at this point you picture a strong, solid Play 1, with you in charge of the entire situation. On the other hand, if you are returning and have chosen Play 2, then you will picture a strong return—one that will create a short ball—and you will picture yourself charging in to take the short ball early, closing for a good volley to win the point.

DEALING WITH INTERRUPTIONS

Suppose you are just about to complete your Reset routine by beginning your serve when something interrupts you. It might be that your opponent engages in a bit of gamesmanship and delays play. Or a ball may roll out on the court. What do you do?

Answer: Start the Three R's all over, completing each R, even though you might make the Release and the Review quite short.

For example, suppose your opponent turns to the crowd and makes a joke just as you are about to serve. Here is what you can do:

- *Release:* Walk away from the service line, perhaps saying to yourself, "What a jerk!"
- *STOP*
- *Review:* "He thinks this will throw me off, but I won't let it happen. My plan was to kick the serve high to his backhand, and that's still what I'm going to do. I'll do an especially good Reset routine, with a good deep breath to focus, and I'll keep this from throwing me off."
- *STOP*
- *Reset:* Do the Reset routine that was interrupted—from the beginning. Take the deep breath, form the image, bounce the ball, whatever you were going to do.

The key is to use the Reset routine as your own entry for the next point, and not let anyone take it away from you. They may interrupt it—but you will simply step back and move through the Three R's again, using the Release to let go of any frustration that may be present, the Review to analyze the interruption and make your plan, and the Reset routine to get ready to play the point.

It's natural! Remember that we all have to hit a lot of balls to develop our best shots. And that at some point hitting good shots starts to feel natural. Even more, it feels great to hit solid shots. The same is true of the Three R's between points. After you develop your own sequence, the between-point time becomes your ally, a time to enjoy the good that just happened, or to correct for anything that is not going well. Remember too, that the Three R's is a no-fail system: If you drop your guard and lose it in some way (outburst, discouragement, or choke), you can always recover with a Release, a quick Review, and a Reset routine to bring focus to the next point.

EXERCISES TO HELP YOU RESET

Exercise 1

What Reset routines do you characteristically perform when serving? How about when returning?

Exercise 2

Check items on the lists that follow to identify elements of your own Reset routine.

I Will:	I Will Avoid:
When serving: ☐ Step to the line. ☐ Call score. ☐ Relax with a deep breath. ☐ Bounce the ball ___ times. ☐ Imagine a great serve to start a great point. ☐ Begin serve. When returning: ☐ Step to the line. ☐ Check score. ☐ Get "on my toes." ☐ Jump on the return.	☐ Letting anyone keep me from doing my Reset routine. ☐ Skipping my Reset routine.

(continued)

Exercise 2, (continued)

I Will:	I Will Avoid:
If Underaroused, ☐ Rev up by slapping my leg, saying "Come on" or something else to get me going. Chosen phrase: _____	If Underaroused, ☐ Drifting into next point with no energy or focus.

Considering the items you have checked, write out a summary of your own standard Reset routines for serving and returning.

_____

_____

_____

Summary of service Reset routine:

_____

_____

_____

Summary of return Reset routine:

_____

_____

_____

Exercise 3

Practice your Reset routine when playing with a friend. Have an observer code your behavior from a live match or from a videotape using the Coding Manual in chapter 7.

JOHN McENROE

From 1981 to 1984 John McEnroe ranked as the No. 1 player in tennis and is still praised for a nearly perfect technique. McEnroe claimed 77 singles titles, including four U.S. Open championships and three Wimbledon titles during his 16-year professional career.

Considered one of the foremost doubles players in the history of the sport, he won the doubles crown five times at Wimbledon and four times at the U.S. Open. He won the French Open mixed doubles title in 1979 with Mary Carillo.

Known for loud negative Releases when his game wasn't going well, he maintained clear internal focus and stayed on top of his game by having a strong Review after missed shots. Additionally, McEnroe employed a distinctive Reset routine of pulling his shirt up over his shoulder before serving.

McEnroe is now a match analyst for CBS and has done tennis match analysis for the USA Network and NBC.

John McEnroe was born in Wiesbaden, Germany, on February 10, 1959, and divides his time between New York and Malibu, California. He is active with The Safe Passage Foundation, founded by the late Arthur Ashe, which provides 6,000 inner-city youths with tennis instruction and educational counseling.

John McEnroe

© Tommy Hindley

CHAPTER **6** *Competing With the Three R's*

Now that you know how the Three R's system works, and now that you have a picture of what your own Releases, Reviews, and Reset routines can be, this chapter will help you apply the Three R's to standard tennis situations. Then we will show how to apply the system to standard tennis disasters. As you read through our solutions to problems such as tantrums, choking, and tanking, you may find some that apply to you or to someone you know. The good news is that you can use the Three R's between points to counter every one of these situations. A table at the end of the chapter summarizes the main points, showing the symptoms and the results you can get when you apply the Three R's as a solution.

TENNIS APPLICATIONS

A moment's thought reveals that there are at least three standard situations to which you can apply the Three R's in tennis: Between points, at changeovers, and between matches. Let's take a look at each.

Between Points

We've been talking about using the Three R's between points all along, so here we will simply remind you that the idea is to do some version of the Three R's before every point. This means that in the early going of a match, perhaps when you are playing well, the Three R's will be more streamlined, shorter, and feel like no big deal. Do not skip the routine, however. We have seen players invite disastrous mental lapses by skipping the Three R's, or by trying to apply the system only on the two to three big points in the match. This does not work. You need to make it a part of your ongoing between-point experience.

Try something like this. If you are playing well, the Release can be quiet, positive, affirmative. Just think to yourself: "You're doing great. Keep it up." The Review need be no more than a quick "Play 1." (Or Play 2 or Play 3, of course.) But the Reset routine will be the same as in difficult situations: Look to the opposite

court, take a deep breath to relax and let it out, form an image, bounce the ball, and serve. This takes very little time, and the constant repetition is what gives it its strength.

When things are going badly, you may take more time. The Release is more critical and important to you because it gives you a chance to let go of tremendously negative feelings in a constructive way. In intense situations, such as when you are in a critical game in the final set, it will be important to use the Review to assess the situation and to pick the best play—still without going through a lot of thinking, but without shortchanging yourself, either. And the Reset routine will come into its own. All that repetition during practice and good times on the court will add up to something you can use to focus your thoughts and images and concentrate even under conditions of extreme stress or fatigue.

Changeovers

You have 90 seconds at the changeover, and the question is what to do with it. Simply walking to the side, sitting down, toweling off, and drinking fluids is an important part of most players' changeover procedures. Allow your mind, heart, and feelings to go through the Three R's as you go through the changeover. Release feelings and thoughts. The Release might be about your play: Being aware that you are playing well or playing badly. Or use the Release as an outlet to take a break: Look at the crowd, think about what this match means to you, or anything else that may be on your mind. Release and allow these thoughts and feelings to come out. Then end them with the STOP technique, and move to Review: "What do I need to do next?" During a changeover, you can even pull out your play book and Review your game plan. Then continue into a changeover Reset routine that includes more relaxation. Put a cold (or hot) towel on the back of your neck if you are extremely fatigued. Close your eyes. Use mental imagery of what you will be doing next. Then get up and move to the other side to begin play. Notice that if you have done the first two of the Three R's thoroughly enough while on the bench, then you may well move to the active Reset routine as you walk over to begin your serve (skipping the Release and Review that you normally would do while in transit between points).

Before Matches

As you get ready for a big tournament, your mind might be filled with all kinds of debilitating and frightening thoughts: "What if I don't play as well as I need to? What will happen to my rankings? Should I look at the draw, or will that make me think too far ahead? This person is really good."

A multitude of other thoughts or experiences may come your way to make your life difficult, increase anxiety, interfere with practice, or interfere with sleep as you prepare for a match. The solution can be to apply the Three R's whenever you face any distraction between matches. Let's have a look at how you might do this.

You are one week away from a major tournament that could have an important effect on your rankings. Someone makes a comment about the opponent you might draw in the first round, and you begin to get uptight and nervous about the situation. Your mind races to thoughts about not wanting to draw a particular player in the first round, and a fear that you will. You chastise yourself for being afraid of this opponent, though in your heart of hearts you feel afraid, and that makes it worse. What can you do?

Release the feelings by acknowledging that this is what you are thinking. Notice the mental pictures you have of the draw sheet and the name of the opponent, and notice the feelings in your stomach as you think of playing that person. Allow the feelings to occur. Release them into your consciousness. Then STOP yourself and move to a Review.

During the Review, reflect critically on what is going on. Say to yourself, "Look at me thinking about the draw sheet, and my opponent, and making myself uptight by doing so. I'm thinking more about the rankings and all these other things than I am about what it takes to win. Let me ask myself right now what does it take to beat this person? Well, the same thing it takes to beat anybody else. I have to watch the ball, play the ball, execute my game plan, and play each point one at a time. That's what I need to do. Also, I'm going to have to get more first serves in against this person than somebody else because this one likes to punish second serves. So, I need to work on first serves this week, and beyond that, simply follow my game plan. I will work on that all week."

Then STOP the Review. Review is good and useful, but not when you go around and around over the same ideas. Think it through once, then start a Reset routine. Develop a specialized Reset for this sort of situation—perhaps deep muscle relaxation and visualization of what you want to do in the match, or perhaps reading, watching a movie, or simply taking a deep breath and going on with the business at hand. If you are in class and about to complete an algebra assignment when the upcoming match intrudes on your thoughts, both your tennis and your grade will benefit if you can get back to the algebra assignment without a lot of wasted energy.

When you have mapped out a constructive action, take that action at once if you can. If you are getting ready to go out and play, carry out what you said you would do. Work on first serves, work

on watching the ball, work on playing the ball at all costs without getting into distracting thoughts. If you are in class or at work or otherwise tied up when you start thinking about the match, make the commitment or even write a note to yourself that says you will work on first serves and playing the ball this afternoon, but right now you are going to complete the other work in front of you.

The same techniques will come in handy during delays once the tournament gets started. If it's raining or there's something else keeping you off the court, do whatever you find useful to help yourself relax, maintain concentration, and save energy. Eat, rest, listen to music, read, play cards, or watch a movie in your room. When the upcoming match intrudes on your thoughts, run through the Three R's briefly and return to your placeholding activity. Avoid the spiraling tension of endless worry or negative thinking.

TROUBLESHOOTING

You can use the Three R's as an appropriate channel for any thought, feeling, or challenge that may come your way in getting ready for a match. The Three R's system is the opposite of denial:

You don't block out what is happening and keep yourself from learning from it. Instead, you treat the disruption and the accompanying thought or feeling as a friend. Something floats into your consciousness and makes you think about the match, even though it causes you anxiety to do so. You allow it to happen (this is the Release), and then you STOP it. Then you move to a Review to analyze the situation and decide how you can learn from it. You make a commitment right here and right now to do one or two correct things this week to help get ready for the match. This is the very same as saying to yourself Play 1, Play 2, or Play 3 during the between-point use of the Three R's. And then you STOP the Review and get on with your life.

Tantrums

"Excuse me, but this situation is so frustrating, I think I'll just destroy everything in sight."

Everyone experiences frustrations at one time or another. Some obstacle gets in the way of a goal. As a matter of fact, that is what competition is all about: Trying to block the progress of an opponent while the opponent is trying to do the same to you. How about when you frustrate yourself? What if your own poor play or unforced errors make you so mad that you cannot control your feelings? Every tennis player has seen extreme examples of this. Angry outbursts expressed at anything in sight: the ball (the ball you strike in anger could hit a spectator); inanimate objects (John McEnroe once kicked a water cooler off its stand, sending water and ice all over the side of the court); your opponent (if you are susceptible to tantrums, then you know what it feels like to get into a verbal if not a physical altercation with an opponent). A player Robert knows once got so mad after being cheated repeatedly by line judges and umpires in a small town that the player walked over and shook the umpire's chair so violently that the umpire fell out of the chair and broke his arm. Tournament officials had to intervene, ending the match, and telling the player to leave town before somebody killed him.

Tantrums are simply behavioral expressions of deeply felt angry feelings. At its heart, anger reflects a view that what is happening

right now is simply "not right, not just, and I'm not gonna take it anymore!" When a tennis player gets angry, the player is usually angry at himself or herself, although the anger may be directed at someone outside—a referee for a bad line call, an opponent for cheating, or a photographer or a reporter for causing a distraction in the stands.

Good News and Bad News

While most people do not recognize it, the good part about anger is that it shows that you care about what is happening to you. If you did not set high standards for yourself, and if you did not have a sense of justice about the rules of the game, you would not care if you played badly; you would not care if your opponent cheated; you would not care if someone interfered with play. So at its heart, it is a positive sign that you are paying close enough attention to yourself, your opponent, and the entire situation to notice violations, and to notice that you are not playing up to your own standard of excellence.

The negative, of course, is that you can get so angry that the emotion gets out of control. Your anger takes over and totally obliterates any chance of playing well. Anger turns to a destructive tantrum when you abuse equipment and people so badly that you receive a code violation (or are disqualified altogether), or when you lose track of what you are trying to do during the point and your feelings interfere with your shots. Every tennis player knows that there is a fine line between anger that motivates and energizes—anger that is under control—and anger that goes over the line.

Three R's Check

Have you truly defined what a good Release will be for you? In the best of all worlds, how do you want to let your feelings out? If

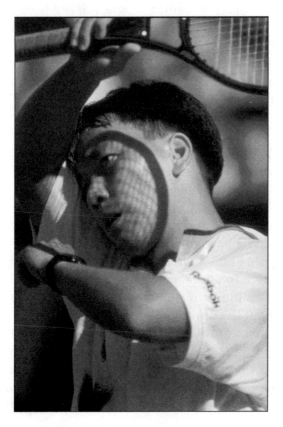

you have not given this enough attention, then you will be likely to fall into old patterns of swearing, abusing rackets, and the like. Once you have practiced a solid Release, remember that even if you should lose it and fall into bad behavior, you can use the STOP technique any time you want. After you do that, it is critical that you engage in some sort of standard Review behavior (for example, switching your racket to your nonplaying hand) to cue yourself into the next phase. After the Review, use the Reset routine as a way to put yourself into a relaxed state for the next point.

Choking

"I'm so nervous right now, I believe I'll just tighten all my muscles so I can't hit this shot well at all. Also, I think I'll desert my game plan, try to protect my lead, and, eventually, I guess, I'll lose."

No one says it just this way, but that is what a choke is: nervousness that becomes debilitating. Choking begins with thinking about everything other than hitting the ball and executing the game plan. A player will think about how important this match is in terms of rankings or who might be watching, or indulge in internal monologues like this: "I was up 5–1, and now the score is 5–5. I can't believe I let it go!"

At the heart of choking is nervousness or anxiety—psychologists' words for fear about consequences. "I'm afraid I might lose this match. I get worried that I will not be able to break serve. I am anxious about my first serve; it's going to desert me. My coach will think badly of me if I do not beat this person (whom I should beat, based on past performance)." As with the feeling of anger that underlies a tantrum, the feeling of anxiety underlying a choke is one that can be used to your advantage if you are able to understand the feeling and channel it in a constructive direction.

It is a strength to appreciate the importance of getting your first serve in (not giving your opponent a chance to unload on a weak second serve). It is a plus to want to win a match and improve your rankings, or to avoid blowing a 5–1 lead. The fact that you care about such things is an indication that you are aware of the situation, which is the first requirement for doing something about it.

The negative is that you can get so anxious that the feeling runs away with you and takes over the situation. When this happens, you become so nervous, so anxious, that your muscles tighten up and you are unable to execute shots. Most tennis players have had this happen at one time or another. The standard tennis term for this situation is that you start to "push," barely blocking the ball back instead of executing the shots with fluid strokes that have energy, power, and direction. Just as the word *choke* conjures up an image of air being closed off from your windpipe, choke also indicates a tightening of muscles, constricting of blood flow, and an inability to hit the ball properly.

Three R's Check

What can you do to use this heightened awareness and concern constructively, and keep anxiety from turning into choking? The Three R's response to a choke involves a Release of tension (perhaps with humor), a Review of the causes (for example, "Here I go thinking about how *huge* this match is to me, instead of executing my shots"), and a relaxing Reset routine (very deep breath, let out slowly, and then my image and ball bounce). This use of the Three R's lets you understand what is happening, perhaps express the feelings with humor, and then leave them behind by getting back to the matter at hand with a new and improved focus on watching the ball or executing the game plan.

Tanking

"I've had enough of this, thank you. If I can't play any better than this, then I quit."

Tanking is the ultimate control maneuver. The logic seems to go something like this: "Sure, I'm playing badly and you're playing pretty well; you're about to beat me. But I won't let you beat me. I will not give you that kind of control over my life. How will I accomplish this? Simple, I will quit playing. Oh, I will go through the motions, but I will show you and everybody else that I'm not really trying. I feel so bad about what has happened and is now happening that I will not tolerate it. I would rather have you see me as a depressed and discouraged player, one who gave up and let you take it, than allow you to beat me. My ego and heart, to be quite honest about it, won't stand for you beating me, so, I will not let you do it. I quit."

If you think about competition as a matter of fighting and attempting to control the outcome, then the psychology of the tank is understandable. It is a desperate move, however, one in which the player demeans himself or herself in an attempt to retain some semblance of self-esteem. To further complicate the matter, a tank can sometimes turn a match around (thereby reinforcing the tank behavior). Your opponent, seeing that you have quit, lets down. You hit freely (after all, there's nothing to lose now) and start to win some points, or a game or two. An experience or two like this and the strategy may be reinforced enough that it unconsciously becomes a part of your approach to difficult situations.

As with anger and anxiety, tanking indicates discouragement about the situation, a form of on-court depression. If giving up becomes a part of your standard response, then it will hurt you more than it will help you over the course of your tennis career. Tennis is one of the few sports where the clock does not run out. There is always a chance to come back. We remember Jimmy Connors' comeback victory over Michael Pernfors at Wimbledon. Having lost the first two sets, Connors was down 1–4 in the third. To the amazement of all, Jimmy hung in there to win the third set, and the fourth, and eventually to take the match in five sets. How did he do it? By blocking out the score, and playing the ball, one point at a time.

Three R's Check

How can you turn negative feelings of discouragement in a constructive direction? Use the Three R's to make an adjustment in your game plan, and to ride the situation through. Remember that it does not take much to begin forcing errors in your opponent, and doing so transfers the negative feelings to the other side of the court.

Allow the Review phase to turn things around by giving yourself clear instructions to focus on the ball, or do something else very concrete. Focus on executing your shots (perhaps "execute" could be a code word during Review), or focus on calling Play 1 or Play 2. One of the most disastrous parts of the tank occurs when the mind wanders, but you can counter this by focusing concretely on what you are going to do, calling to mind your predetermined game plan during the Review phase.

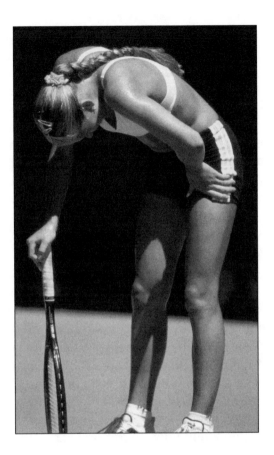

Distracted

"I think I'll just tune in on anything I please—that weird guy in the stands, what's happening on the next court, my date tonight. After all, I'm special: I don't really have to watch the ball or execute my game plan. I can do several things at once."

In its most positive form, distraction means that you are a well-rounded human being. After all, you were not born simply to hit a tennis ball and execute a game plan. You have a life! You care about your relationships, your car, your bank balance, your friends, the people in the stands, and the newspaper and TV reporters. None of these concerns is bad. The problem arises when you think about them in the middle of a point, or as you are getting ready to serve to win a tiebreaker.

Every tennis player has run into distractions. Some come from inside, as when you let your mind drift, seemingly a willful act.

Others come from the outside, such as a loud noise, an airplane flying overhead, a ball that rolls onto your court. An opponent goes through antics that generate laughter from the sidelines, or a line judge makes a bad call against you.

As with all the other emotions, at the heart of distractibility is the fact that you are a human being. People do pay attention to what is happening around them. It becomes a problem only when you pay too much attention. It will not help to be thinking about the bad line call or the planes overhead as you make the toss on your second serve at a crucial point in a tiebreaker.

Three R's Check

How can you keep distractions from interfering with your own ability to perform? How can you move from a distraction to a mental focus on watching the ball, executing shots, and completing the game plan?

Try exaggerating the wandering of your mind during the Release. ("I can't serve at all, *and* I've got to get my car washed today too!") Let it go, and then use the STOP technique to end the distraction and use the Review to get your head back into the game ("Come on! Play! Get in!"). Remember, too, the rev-up version of the Reset routine, which you might need to get yourself back into the game when you are distracted.

No Motivation Today

"You know, tennis is a wonderful game, and I'm committed to competitive play. But I just don't care about any of it today."

No one can stay totally focused on the task at hand indefinitely. Some players have a tough time motivating themselves to practice, then do quite well during matches. Others cannot get "up" when they feel they really ought to. What are your feelings telling you when you cannot get motivated to perform? It might be that your priorities are off. You might have invested too much time, effort, and money in your sport, to the exclusion of other interests and priorities, and your unmotivated play is your body's way of getting the message through to your mind. Or perhaps you are burned out, overextended, or mentally exhausted. Or maybe it really is just that on this particular day and at this particular moment you cannot get your head into the match. Sometimes you get by with low motivation, and other times you pay a price. How about losing to someone that you should beat? You walk off the court with the knowledge that the other player wanted it more than you did.

Three R's Check

Use the Three R's to motivate yourself while on the court—and in practice. During your Release, allow the thoughts and words that you are "not motivated" to come out, to be Released into your consciousness. Perhaps chastise yourself or make fun of yourself a bit, but do not become so negative that you drag yourself down even further. Say, "Okay, maybe I'm not motivated to play—but I'm on the court. Do I really want to lose to this person?" Then use the STOP word, and kick in your "pump-up" positive statements during the Review, followed by a solid rev-up Reset routine. Revving up can be your best friend when you are feeling lethargic and unmotivated.

Uneven Performance

"Sometimes I'm good, and sometimes I'm bad. I can never predict what it will be!"

Let's start with the positive part of uneven performance: At least you are good some of the time! As with any athlete, your goal now is to increase the number of times you do well, and decrease the number of times you do poorly. Your problem may be that you make too many unforced errors, losing points and even games, not because your opponent has done anything great, but because you have overhit or lost concentration. At the heart of the problem is an inability to correct errors immediately and keep them from turning into a downward spiral.

Three R's Check

What can you do between points to maintain intensity, focus, and concentration to close out opponents and reduce unforced errors? Use the Three R's to fix errors as they occur. Use the Review especially as a time to analyze what just happened. For example, did you take your eye off the ball, or watch your opponent charging the net instead of watching the ball as you got ready to pass? Picture what you would like to do next as a part of your Review. In this way the Three R's will allow you to solve the problem of uneven performance by fixing errors as they occur.

If you have fallen behind, set a goal during the Review to execute your shots until you get to a point where you are back in the game. You can resist the tendency to overgeneralize and catastrophize about your play (after having blown a few shots) by making a solid Review of the past to see exactly what happened, and then putting the game plan or code word phrases into play to correct your errors.

Losing the Lead

"I go great until it gets to 5–1, then my opponent comes back to win the set. I can't believe I let that happen!"

Sometimes you simply let down, relax too much, thinking you have a cushion of a few games. As all teaching pros know, this can be a disaster. The psychology of a 5–1 lead is that the player in the lead tends to relax; it's always tempting to coast through a game when you seem to be so far ahead: "Let's see, even if she breaks me, and then I hold . . ." Meanwhile, the opponent sees that there is nothing to lose and begins to hit out on the ball, lifting the level of play. This combination can change the score quickly in the favor of the player who has been behind.

Three R's Check

How can you keep up the intensity and focus when you are ahead so as to close out the match and ride through an opponent whose level of play is starting to climb?

During the Review, remind yourself to play as if you are in a tiebreaker, even though you are up 5–1. Or use any other phrase that will surely make you focus. (For example, during the Review, pretend that you are *down* 1–5). Make sure you do this in every between-point interval. It will become another habit, and one that will increase your chance of keeping in focus when you run into conditions that tempt you to let down.

RUNAWAY FEELINGS AND THOUGHTS

Each of the situations we've discussed begins with an absolutely normal feeling, although one with the potential to escalate into an abnormal reaction. Remember that the danger lies not in simply feeling anger, frustration, anxiety, discouragement, or boredom, but in giving these feelings free rein to control you on the court. Think of it this way: These feelings serve as a gauge to let you evaluate a situation. It is entirely good that your mind is working to evaluate the situation. As table 6.1 shows, by understanding the feelings, you can channel them in a positive direction. As we all know, the real disasters occur when these feelings escalate unchecked and turn into behavior that hurts your performance. By using the Three R's, you can take advantage of these feelings instead. The Release gives an outlet. The Review gives understanding and a plan for recovery. And the Reset routine brings steady focus before the next point. The two STOPs (after the Release and after the Review) protect against the runaway threat of heavy-duty emotion.

Table 6.1   The Three R's Solution

Symptom	Outcomes		How
	No Three R's	*Three R's*	
Tantrums	Anger spills into next point, leading to unforced errors, code violations, lack of control.	Anger channeled and stopped from spilling into next point; energy focused on next ball and channeled into hitting next ball.	Constructive Releases replace destructive ones; STOP technique to end Release and move to Review; Review to analyze what to do next; Reset routine to bring relaxation and focus to next ball.

(continued)

Table 6.1, (continued)

Symptom	Outcomes		How
	No Three R's	*Three R's*	
Choking	Anxiety leads to tight muscles, choke, poor performance, forgetting game plan.	Release of tension permits new perspective through Review phase (stopping overgeneralizing and catastrophizing); increased focus on next point; relaxed anticipation of next ball.	Use of humor in Release phase; analysis of self-defeating talk in Review; code phrases to focus on this ball (not necessarily the outcome of the match); Reset routine with built-in relaxation to prepare to execute next point.
Tanking	Discouragement, low intensity, "feel like made of lead," cannot move.	Negative transformed into constructive plan; focus on the ball and give concrete instructions on what to do next.	Release lets out the negative, and STOP keeps it from getting out of hand; Review allows return to game plan; Reset routine allows for programmed preparation for next ball (instead of falling prey to the weight of depressing feelings).
Distracted	Focus on irrelevant activity, poor concentration, unforced errors.	Mind may wander initially, but not forever (STOP!); head gets back in game and back to game plan.	Distraction can form part of Release, but STOP ends distracting thoughts; behavioral cue begins Review; reminder of preplanned game plan occurs during Review; Reset routine keeps mind and heart on track for next point.

(continued)

Table 6.1, (continued)

Symptom	Outcomes		How
	No Three R's	*Three R's*	
Not motivated	Low intensity; head not in game—leads to lost points and games.	Stimulated, ready for next point.	Code words during Review (and behavioral cue during Review) bring game plan to fore and prepare for next ball; Reset routine provides focus for next point.
Uneven performance	Unforced errors; lost points and games; more discouragement.	Errors get corrected immediately, so problems become strengths.	Use of "fix it" Release; game plan approach to Review phase makes for simpler instructions on the court; positive image allows for focus on "how to" as opposed to "wrong way" in preparation for next ball.
Losing the lead	Lack of attention when far ahead (5–1) lets opponent back in the match, sometimes resulting in lost set or match.	Focus of Three R's system allows you to maintain intensity and level of play to close out match.	Verbal instructions during Review phase keep you bearing down and playing as if you are behind, or as if you are in a tiebreaker (where each point counts as holding serve or a mini break).

STEFFI GRAF

Steffi Graf was 4 years old when she began playing tennis, and turned pro when she was 13 in 1982. By the end of 1996, she placed first in season-ending singles rankings for the eighth time since 1982. Graff won seven titles in 1996 including Wimbledon, the U.S. Open, the German Open, Lipton, Indian Wells, and Roland Garros, collecting $2,665,706 in prize money and bringing her career title record to 102. She earned her 100th singles title at 1996 Wimbledon, becoming the third woman in the Open Era (behind Navratilova and Evert) to pass that milestone.

Graf uses tight concentration and tremendous speed to maintain an edge over her opponents. She has a quiet demeanor on the court, not letting line calls or botched shots crowd in on her game focus. She plays point by point, running everything down and not allowing any loose points to get past her.

Steffi Graf was born in Bruhl, Germany, on June 14, 1969. She divides her time between Bruhl and New York City. She loves animals and enjoys all kinds of music. She appreciates impressionist and modern art and passes time off the court shooting photographs, reading, and playing cards. She helped found the Steffi Graf Youth Tennis Center, which was dedicated in October 1991 in Leipzig, Germany.

© Tommy Hindley

Steffi Graf

CHAPTER 7 *Practicing With the Three R's*

Develop your own customized Three R's—and then practice it so that it becomes as much a part of your game as your forehand, backhand, overhead, serve, volley, and return of serve. Just as it takes hitting a lot of practice balls to groove a stroke, it takes a lot of repetition to settle into your own customized Three R's. Practice during regular workouts (and even when simply thinking about your tennis game) and you will see immediate results when you get into match play, especially in close situations when everything is on the line in one or two points. This chapter gives our six-step practice plan for building the Three R's into your overall game.

STEP ONE: WRITE OUT YOUR OWN THREE R'S

By completing the worksheets in chapters 3, 4, and 5, you already have a draft version of what your Three R's will look like. If you have not done so already, fill out these checklists. Then summarize them in the Three R's worksheet in this section. This is your working draft of what you would like to see yourself doing between points. Literally see, in your mind's eye—imagine a videotape of one of your matches, and watch yourself doing these things. When you look comfortable and happy, you will know what your own Three R's should look like. It is the same as with your forehand. When you are executing the stroke well, you will have a good shoulder turn, you will strike the ball ahead of you and follow through. If you get jammed (because you turned too late, did not move your feet, or because your opponent hit a tremendous shot), then the forehand will not work so well. But you will not be able to diagnose this in the forehand unless you have the ideal shot in mind already, and have grooved it in practice. The same is true of the Three R's. What you write in the worksheet is your ideal Three R's, the pattern you aspire to go through between every point.

STEP TWO: WRITE OUT YOUR GAME PLAN

Unlike athletes in many other sports (basketball, football, baseball), tennis players do not usually call plays for themselves before they begin a point. Instead, they think the situation over between points, decide what to do, and then attempt to do it. As a part of the Three R's Sport Psychology System, we suggest that players pick one of the three preplanned Plays first presented in chapter 3, and then implement that Play during the point. The obvious advantage of this approach is that it simplifies playmaking, so that players can spend less time thinking. This is especially important when fatigue sets in. It saves a lot of mental effort if you can keep the number of big decisions you must make on the court to a minimum, adjusting your plan only for weaknesses you spot in your opponent during the match. The objective is to implement a game plan, and to do it well. These standard Plays will help you develop your personal game plan, lock it in with mental imagery practice, and apply it in match play.

Play 1: "I'm Coming In—Now!"

This is the most aggressive play in tennis. On serve, it means serve and volley: After this good serve, I'm coming in to hit a volley, after which I will close for a cut-off volley to win the point. I will be ready for an overhead. All movement forward to the net.

Returning, I plan either to chip and charge, or to hit the return solid and come in immediately.

The whole idea behind Play 1 is to achieve the advantage of court position (taking the net), and then win the point.

Three R's Worksheet

RELEASE

I Will:

- [ ] Make corrective comments: "Stay down!" "Watch the ball!"
- [ ] Say "come on," "yes," "that's it" (After doing well on a big point).
- [ ] Use "fist pump."
- [ ] Use humor after an error.
- [ ] Imitate the good shot to override the bad one.
- [ ] Do all of this in a "quiet sort of way."
- [ ] Do all of this in a "flamboyant sort of way."
- [ ] Compliment my opponent: "Too good," "Great shot," applaud with racket.
- [ ] Other (list):

_____

_____

_____

I Will Avoid:

- [ ] Global negatives: "You're so bad," "You Stink."
- [ ] Profanity.
- [ ] Racket, ball, people abuse.
- [ ] Other (list):

_____

_____

_____

STOP

Looking at the items you have checked, and in light of your own history with Releases, write a summary you want to include in your Release phase.

_____

_____

_____

REVIEW

I Will:

- ☐ Switch racket to nonplaying hand to start Review.
- ☐ Walk confidently (shoulders back, head up).
- ☐ Look at my strings as I think.
- ☐ Ask the "coach questions."
  - ☐ What just happened?
  - ☐ Why did I win the point?
  - ☐ Why did I lose the point?
  - ☐ Am I doing my game plan?
  - ☐ Am I playing my opponent's weakness?
  - ☐ What do I need to do next?
- ☐ Call "Play 1," "Play 2," or "Play 3."
- ☐ Say my code words (such as "Watch the ball," "Be strong," "Play the ball," "Get in!").
- ☐ **Relax** with deep breathing.
- ☐ Other (list):

_____

_____

_____

I Will Avoid:

- ☐ Skipping the **Review**.
- ☐ Looking just at the bad.
- ☐ Forgetting my game plan.
- ☐ Looking at coach (parents) for help.
- ☐ Other (list):

_____

_____

_____

Looking at the items you have checked, write down a summary of what would be an ideal Review for you between points.

_____

_____

_____

RESET ROUTINE

I Will:	**I Will Avoid:**
If Overaroused,	If Overaroused,
When serving:	☐ Letting anyone keep me from doing my Reset routine.
☐ Step to the line.	
☐ Call score.	☐ Skipping my Reset routine.
☐ **Relax** with a deep breath.	
☐ Bounce the ball a set number of times.	
☐ Imagine a great serve to start a great point.	
☐ Begin motion.	
When returning:	
☐ Step to the line.	
☐ Check score.	
☐ Get "on my toes."	
☐ Jump on the return.	
If Underaroused,	If Underaroused,
☐ **Rev up** by slapping my leg, saying "Come on" or something else to get me going. Chosen phrase: _____	☐ Drifting into next point with no energy or focus.

(continued)

Three R's Worksheet, (continued)

PLAY
Considering the items you have checked, write out a summary of your own standard Reset routines for serving and returning.

_____

_____

_____

Summary of service Reset routine:

_____

_____

_____

Summary of return Reset routine:

_____

_____

_____

Play 2: "Work the Point, and Then Come In!"

Play 2 involves working the point with solid ground strokes, trying to create a short ball so that I can come in immediately on the short ball. It requires solid ground strokes to move my opponent around, and it requires hitting an effective approach shot so I can get in. Once I get in to hit a volley, the goal is the same as for Play 1: Cut off the volley or crunch the overhead to win the point.

The theory behind Play 2 is the same as behind Play 1: If I have the advantage of court position at the net, I increase my chances of winning the point; conversely, if I let my opponent get in, then my opponent has the advantage, so I want to get in first. Play 2 works on returning or serving situations.

Play 3: "Win From the Baseline."

This is used when a player has especially strong ground strokes that can overpower an opponent; it also can be used if a player needs to regain confidence so as to do Play 1 or Play 2 after getting "back in the game." Using Play 3, you work the point, attempting to run your opponent all over the court, working the point until you generate an error or hit a winner.

Think through key matches and see if you are most effective when doing Play 1, Play 2, Play 3, or combinations. Identify specific matches and specific points where you were more or less effective. Think of opponents you have played who have beaten you: How did they beat you?

Now, write out your own game plan. For example: I will do Play 1 and Play 2 as my main approach, with Play 3 as backup only if I get in trouble. Also, when serving, I will do more Play 1 than Play 2, especially on key points. In all cases I will think aggressively to implement Play 1 and Play 2, knowing that I increase my chances of winning if I can take the net from my opponent.

STEP THREE: DO IMAGERY TRAINING

The purpose of imagery training is to give you an experience of yourself implementing the Three R's (including Review of your game plan) before you get on the court. There are many ways to do imagery training, some informal and others that take a specific amount of time. Daydreaming is actually imagery training. The question is, do you daydream about negative things or do you daydream about things that are positive and contribute to your overall success? Begin right now using any daydreaming time to picture yourself as strong and confident between points, Releasing negatives as they occur, Reviewing your game plan, and Resetting with a routine that improves your performance on the next point. Cultivate this image of yourself as often as you can.

You can increase the power of these images through practice imagery training. Try this 10-minute exercise twice a day for two weeks:

- Find a comfortable spot where you will not be interrupted. Relax with deep breathing or deep muscle relaxation. (For tips on these techniques, see chapter 2.) Go through the following mental pictures.

- Picture yourself playing the best match of your life. (It could be a real match or an imaginary one.) As you do so, use all five of your senses. Picture the ball as you hit it. Hear the sound of your feet as you turn and run to meet the ball. Feel the great stroke as you follow through, never taking your eyes off the ball.

- Picture yourself playing points, and between points doing the Three R's, and focusing on the choice of Play 1 or Play 2.
- Play out each point using Play 1 or Play 2, closing it with a victory at the net (cut off volley or overhead). Enjoy the feeling of successful play.
- Continue this and play out several games—even an entire set.
- Close the imagery by winning the set and match.
- Continue to relax and soak in the images and feelings of playing aggressive tennis, getting to the net using Play 1 and Play 2, and winning.
- Stop the exercise by opening your eyes and emerging confident and relaxed.
- Repeat this twice a day for one week, and then once a day for a week.

If you do imagery training like this and then combine it with daydreaming, you will effectively increase your practice time. It is almost as if you are getting extra opportunities to become a strong tennis player. Players and coaches have found that there is

nothing to compare with imagery training combined with focused practice of hitting the ball on the court to improve performance.

STEP FOUR:
CHART YOUR THREE R'S IN PRACTICE

Now comes the opportunity to complete the Three R's during practice. Most of us were trained to hit as many balls as we could; we tend to think of practice as a time when hitting the ball is the most important thing. We often rush through practice games as if what we do between points does not really matter much. If you want to develop your focus between points, however, treat every between-point opportunity in practice as a chance to use the Three R's. Granted, in some drills the idea is to hit many balls quickly and not regroup between points. On the other hand, such drills— useful as they are—shouldn't take up your whole practice session. Outside of speed drills, create as many opportunities as you can to practice the Three R's between times when you hit the ball. For example, you can:

- Set up tiebreakers, single games, or games to 5 or 10 points and treat them as game situations in which you use the Three R's between points.

- Slow down your activity during some drills for backhands, forehands, and other shots, and make sure to complete a brief Three R's—especially Review, looking for what to do in order to execute the shot properly if you have just missed one.

- Between specific drills (such as serve and volley drills, or even practicing serves), complete a strong Three R's (Release, Review, and Reset) to make *the next ball you hit* better than the preceding one. We once heard Pete Sampras say that practicing one bucket of serves at a time was enough, and we know that is true, *if* you use the Three R's between serves to learn from one serve to the next.

To capture what you are doing, have someone chart your activity using the Three R's Coding Manual in table 7.1. The coding can be done from videotapes or live action, and will give you solid feedback on what you are doing between points.

Table 7.1 Three R's Coding Manual

This coding system is designed for players, coaches, and researchers to use in evaluating the effectiveness of any player's "between-point" performance in tennis. The coding scheme allows evaluation of Releases, Reviews, and Reset routines, and the intervening STOPs. By coding the Three R's performance for each point, players and coaches can see the link between successful use of the Three R's and success or failure on the "big points" in any match. For example, a player might rush between points, perhaps skipping the Review phase, and thereby let the opponent who could have been closed out back into the match. Or, a player might be frustrated and engage in negative talk as a part of the Release, then neglect to STOP the Release and move to a solid Review—allowing the negative Release to spill into the next point, and interfering with performance.

Coding Instructions

This coding chart is designed for use with either a live match or a videotape. For video, keep the camera running for the entire match, including between points and during changeovers.

Code as follows:

1. Write in the names of the players, and identify the game score in the left column.

2. Identify the "point just played" score in each case. All coding is for between-point behavior that follows the point listed in the left column.

3. Write down brief descriptions of all Release behavior, all Review behavior, and all Reset behavior.

4. In addition, jot down a "+," "–," or "?" to show whether the Release, Review, and Reset were constructive (+), destructive (–), or "can't tell from this observation" (?).

5. At the end, answer the summary questions for player feedback:

   a. To what extent does this player execute constructive Releases? (Give examples.)
   b. Does the player need to replace any negative Releases?
   c. What improvements can you see for the Review portion of the Three R's (for example, switching racket to nonplaying hand as a behavioral indication that the Review is in progress)?
   d. What changes should the player make in the Reset routines?
   e. What can the player do to improve performance on the Three R's (for example, practice matches, coding other tapes)?

(continued)

Table 7.1, (continued)

The Three R's Code Sheet

Player Observed: _____   Opponent: _____   Date: _____

Tournament: _____   Observer: _____

	Release	Review	Reset	Comments
Game Score: Server: Point Just Played:	+ − ?	+ − ?	+ − ?	
Game Score: Server: Point Just Played:	+ − ?	+ − ?	+ − ?	
Game Score: Server: Point Just Played:	+ − ?	+ − ?	+ − ?	
Game Score: Server: Point Just Played:	+ − ?	+ − ?	+ − ?	

STEP FIVE: DISCUSS CHARTING RESULTS

Talk with your coach, another player, or some other knowledge-able person about the results of your charting. Ask the following questions:

- How constructive are my Releases? (Ask for examples of effective and ineffective things you do.)

- Do I need to replace any negative Releases? (Ask for specifics.)

- How could you tell that I'd moved into the Review portion of the Three R's? (You should have a behavioral cue to tell yourself that you're in Review, such as switching the racket to your nonplaying hand. If it's so subtle that an outside observer can't spot it, maybe it needs to be more specific.)

- Does it look like my Reset routine is working? (Ask for improvements you could make.)
- What could I do to improve performance on the Three R's? (You're looking for suggestions on the order of taking part in more practice matches, coding other tapes, and so on, that is, specific things to do.)

STEP SIX: REFINE YOUR THREE R'S AS NEEDED

By writing out your Three R's and your game plan, doing imagery training, charting on the court, and getting feedback, you now have the tools to improve every aspect of your tennis game. The Three R's will help you create opportunities to improve from point to point, instead of melting down if things get bad. Do not be afraid to change things that are not working—but if something isn't broken, then don't change it. As Trogolo has said to many players, "Don't change a winning game plan." The same is true of your Three R's. If it is working, do not change it. On the other hand, if you find that you have been having difficulty, and if you see something you admire in another premier player, perhaps the use of humor during a Release or a positive use of a practice fix-it move to replace a bad shot and correct for an error, then build this into your own Three R's. Experiment and refine your system until it fits with your own style.

THOMAS MUSTER

Thomas "King of Clay" Muster is renowned for his 111–5 record on clay courts, the best consecutive clay court record in Open Era play. Muster won seven ATP tour titles in 1996 and was a semifinalist in the U.S. Open, collecting $2,875,496 in prize money. Also in 1996, he held the No. 1 position in tennis for one week and again for five weeks from March 11–April 14, the first left-hander to hold the No. 1 position since John McEnroe did so in the week of September 2, 1985.

In 1989 he was the first Austrian to reach the Australian Open semifinals and was the first Austrian ever to reach the Top 10. In the same year, only hours after defeating Yannick Noah to reach the final at Key Biscayne, he was struck by a drunken driver and injured his left knee, severing several ligaments. The injury barred him from the final with Ivan Lendl. He returned to tennis less than six months after the accident and was named ATP Tour Comeback Player of the Year in 1990.

Muster has a strong work ethic and has been quoted as saying he "lives for tennis." Much of his success on clay surface is due to his tenacity, and his ability to make his opponents work for every point. His distinctive Reset in the form of running around the baseline before receiving, and a very strong Review allow him to stay with his game plan and bring opponents down, mentally and physically.

Thomas Muster was born in Leibnitz, Austria, on October 2, 1967, and lives in Monaco. He plays drums and enjoys photography, abstract art, and painting.

Thomas Muster

CHAPTER 8 Other Uses of the Three R's

Someone once said that the dangerous thing about walking around with a hammer in your hand is that everything starts to look like a nail. We have to agree, and certainly would not suggest that you apply the Three R's to everything in your life. At the same time, you have probably already figured out that this approach can help you in more areas than just tennis. After learning about this system, some of our players report that they use it successfully in areas as wide-ranging as dealing with test anxiety, conducting intense business negotiations, performing surgical operations or complex lab experiments, or talking to family members about a problem.

This chapter summarizes some applications of the Three R's for other areas of your life. Remember that the psychology of learning suggests that the more ways you find to apply a new skill, the quicker you will learn the skill and the better you will be able to use it. As you read through the following sections, begin to think about applying the Three R's not only in tennis (between points, changeovers, before matches), but also in as many other areas of your life as you can. Success in using the Three R's with tennis will help your golf game and will give you an edge in business as well. Take the old adage, "If you don't use it you lose it," and turn it to your advantage: "The more you use it, the better you get!"

OTHER SPORTS

Most tennis players have played other competitive sports, or have other sports they participate in as a break from tennis. How would the Three R's look if applied to golf, basketball, football, or soccer? Clearly, the Three R's applies to any opportunity for reflection— anything parallel to tennis changeovers or between-point activity. Beyond this, there are some differences and some similarities. Shooting a free throw or kicking a field goal or stepping into the batter's box are all situations in which you can apply the Three R's in virtually the same way as in tennis. All you need are Releases, Reviews, and Reset routines that are specific to the particular sport. For example, a batter stepping up to the plate might get involved in banter with the umpire or opposing catcher as a part of the Release, then turn away to get a sign from the third-base coach as a part of the Review about getting ready to hit the pitch. He might then execute a Reset routine by knocking dirt off his cleats or going through some other apparently casual maneuvers with the bat or with the uniform before stepping into the batter's box.

The more opportunities you have to apply the Three R's, the quicker you will learn to apply the system to your own sport of tennis. How would you apply the Three R's to your golf game? Why not treat the walk to your ball between shots just like a longer version of a tennis between-point interval? If you find yourself thinking too much as you stand over the ball, step back, Release the feelings, conduct your Review away from the ball, and then begin your Reset routine again.

COACHING

Coaches can use the Three R's as a way of helping players understand breakdowns that occur on the court. Instead of simply telling a player to stay positive, or be tough, or block out distractions, you can begin by helping a player understand where the breakdowns occur. Are the Releases too negative? Does the negative talk carry forward and paint the next point? Are there STOPs in the sequence that will put a control on the Release? How about the Review? Does it ask the right questions? Is there any thinking going on at all? Does it have an end point? And finally, examine

the Reset routines to see what suggestions there might be for improvement.

You can use the Three R's as a guide for opportunities to coach players when they split sets, or even on the court (for high school and college matches, when this is allowed). We like to begin by asking the player one question after having split sets: "How did you win that first set?" (Or the second set, whichever the player did win.) If the player answers correctly, for example, "I was relaxed, and kept the ball deep, and got in," then leave it alone, perhaps adding one or two words of encouragement. If the player is wrong about what happened, then give corrective feedback about what you observed that led to success, and then again move to something positive. In these situations, you are simply helping with the Review. It is also useful to allow a player to vent with you, which turns out to be your opportunity for Release. And finally, the Reset routine can include advice about brief relaxation, getting water, eating a banana, or any other set of behaviors that get the player ready to go back in and do the very best. The Three R's can serve as a guide for the entire coaching event between sets.

Coaches can use videotapes of matches to demonstrate different Three R's styles (coding them as illustrated in chapter 7), and encourage players to take notes on what they see in televised matches or in live match play from collegiate and professional players. In all cases the objective is to help players to become aware of the three phases, both in themselves and in other players, and design their own Three R's system.

When breakdowns do occur, as surely they will, the concept is to be precise in the feedback. For example, "Your Reset is outstanding, and you seem to be doing a solid Review, but your Releases are getting way out of hand." Or, "I wonder if you are not shortening the Review too much? I did not notice you switching hands on your racket or giving any other sign that you were starting your Review."

TAKING TESTS

Sue got uptight every time she thought of taking a history exam. Her palms would begin to sweat, her heart would race, and she would get a queasy feeling in her stomach at the very thought of all those names and dates she would have to remember, and of trying to put it all together in an essay. It would get so bad sometimes that she avoided studying altogether, afraid even to open the book. Needless to say, she put off studying until the last minute, crammed as much as she could, and then the whole syndrome would start all over again as she walked in to take the exam. She described herself as a nervous wreck and felt that her anxiety had gone way overboard. Instead of getting her primed to do well, her concern got in the way of her performance.

In applying the Three R's, Sue began to express (to herself and to a friend) her feelings of concern about the exam and treated it the same as a Release in tennis. She would talk about how upset she got, about how her palms would sweat, and of how she was afraid of taking the exam, afraid of failing—wanting a good grade, but fearing she would not be able to do well. Then she applied the STOP technique. She literally told herself to STOP! and began to Review the entire situation critically. She noted that she actually enjoyed some parts of her history study; it was remembering everything that bothered her. She also was not sure how much she had to remember. Would she have to memorize all the names and dates, or could she get by with understanding some of the themes from the lecture? In the Review, she realized that she needed to find out from the teacher what the exact structure of the exam would be. She also realized that, in any case, she would need to be able to develop some memory device to remember names and dates. And finally, she realized that before walking into the room for an exam, she ought to be able to use the relaxation techniques she applied to tennis. In summary, her Review led her to the following game plan:

1. Talk to the teacher to learn the exact nature of the exam and what it would take to get ready for it; as an edge, try to find someone who had taken an exam from this teacher and see what kinds of things the teacher actually did like to include (for example, a lot of names and dates, or not).

2. Get some help from a friend or a counselor on a memory device for remembering names and dates, and practice it daily.

3. Apply deep breathing and muscle relaxation techniques as a way of getting centered before taking the exam.

Sue then turned to a Reset routine that had to do with implementing her game plan in a relaxed and focused manner. When sitting alone in her room, she would do something from the game plan that would help her study at that time, or at least make plans for studying later that evening or the next day. If she was in class, in her car, or on the court, she would remind herself during the Reset that she would apply these measures to her studies when she got home at night. At her desk, she would clear the surface of other books, get something refreshing to drink, and arrange paper and pencil as she started (a study parallel to getting ready to serve in tennis).

Whether in class, on the tennis court, or in her own room, and whether she had an opportunity to study or not, she wrapped up the Three R's with a Reset routine that either let her implement

the best next step (do some studying right now or call a friend to talk about this particular teacher's exams), or let her set the matter aside calmly with the confidence that she would do something useful later. She used the Three R's to learn from the situation, that is, to find out what to study, to make a plan to study it, and then to settle down and study it.

YOUR NEW WORLD

Think of your own life situation and look for other applications, whether at work, at school, in other sports, or at home. The system is simple enough to apply, though you'll need to make adjustments depending on the circumstances. Remember always that the more you apply the Three R's, the stronger you will become—and the more easily the system will flow.

The challenge of sport and of life is that things seldom go according to plan. Indeed, a game plan is really just a way of preparing yourself to deal with a range of adverse circumstances and turn them in the direction you want as often as you can. This means that you should not be surprised when things go wrong. Bad weather, fans who won't be quiet at the right time, and opponents who do everything they can to throw you off are all the order of the day in tennis. Other arenas have their own ranges of obstacles.

The Three R's Sport Psychology System is intended to keep you from simply reacting to these things and letting thoughts and feelings take control of you, and instead allow you to channel your reactions through the Release, then the Review, and finally the Reset routine in preparation for playing the point. Instead of objecting and feeling bad that the world is the way it is, you are saying: "Okay world, I understand how you can be! Bring it on! I have thoughts and feelings about what is going to happen, and I will express them in my Release, then I'll Review critically what has happened, pick the best move in my game plan, and then do a solid Reset routine that prepares me to play as well as I can on the next point."

As we said in the beginning, everyone wants to play in the zone—but the question is: How do I get there more often? The Three R's shows you the way, by helping you to deal with whatever comes your way, learning from mistakes, and channeling your energy into your very best play.

MONICA SELES

What does it take to survive a stabbing, and then return to the game two years later and win the Canadian Open? Monica not only survived the knife attack, but also worked through the ordeal psychologically in order to get back into her sport. She is also mentally tough on the court.

Monica Seles won her first Grand Slam in 1988 at 15 and turned pro shortly thereafter. In 1991, she became the second youngest U.S. Open champion at 17 years and 9 months, following Tracy Austin, the 1979 champion. In 1996, she won five titles, including the Australian and Canadian Open, and was a finalist in the U.S. Open, winning $1,154,499 in prize money. Also in 1996, she played on the United States Olympic team.

On April 30, 1993, when Seles was ranked No. 1, she was stabbed in the back by a fan during a changeover while competing against Magdalena Maleeva in Hamburg. The injury put her out of the game for more than a year, but when she returned, she won the 1995 Canadian Open.

Seles is left-handed and plays with a two-handed forehand and backhand, which keeps her opponents guessing about the angle the ball will take off of her racket. She uses shouts as a negative Release and fist pumps as positive Releases. She rarely gets flustered and has a good Review, which is apparent in her adherence to her game plan.

Monica Seles was born December 2, 1973, in Novi Sad, Yugoslavia. She became a U.S. citizen in 1994. She is coached by her father Karolj, who was a cartoonist and a television director. In her spare time, she volunteers with Special Olympics athletes. She lives in Sarasota, Florida.

© Tommy Hindley

Monica Seles

References

Benson, H. *The Relaxation Response.* New York: Avon, 1976.

Bion, W.R. *Experiences in Groups and Other Papers.* London: Tavistock, 1961.

Cousins, N. *Anatomy of an Illness.* New York: Norton, 1979.

Jacobson, E. *You Must Relax.* New York: McGraw-Hill, 1978.

Loehr, J. "Choking." *World Tennis,* February 1990, pp. 24–27.

Mink, O.G., Mink, B.P., and Owen, K.Q. *Groups That Work.* Englewood Cliffs: Educational Technical Publications, 1987.

Slaikeu, K.A. *Crisis Intervention: A Handbook for Practice and Research* (2nd ed.). Boston: Allyn & Bacon, 1990.

Slaikeu, K.A., and Lawhead, S. *Up From the Ashes: How to Survive and Grow Through Personal Crisis.* Grand Rapids: Zondervan, 1987.

Index

About the Authors

Karl Slaikeu, **PhD**, a lifelong tennis enthusiast, lives in Austin, Texas, and is president of Chorda Conflict Management, Inc. He also offers sport psychology consultation to tennis players at all levels, as well as their families, and conducts workshops and seminars for coaches.

The creator of the 3 R's model, Slaikeu played tennis at the collegiate level and now has two children active in tennis as well.

In his spare time, Slaikeu enjoys reading, trout fishing, and, of course, playing tennis.

Robert **Trogolo** has spent many years as a professional tennis player and coach. After spending several years on the pro tour, he went on to coach players such as Michael Chang, Kevin Curren, and Richey Reneberg. He also coached the Malaysian Davis Cup team.

Through Trogolo Tennis International, Inc.(based in Austin), Trogolo consults tennis clubs and advises players new to the women's and men's pro tennis tours.

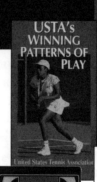
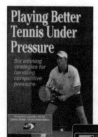